THE SIX GIFTS OF
HOSPITALITY

Patsy Smith

THE SIX GIFTS OF
HOSPITALITY

LAUREL S. SEWELL

Gospel Advocate Company
Nashville, Tennessee

Published by Gospel Advocate Co.
1006 Elm Hill Pike, Nashville, TN 37210
http://www.gospeladvocate.com

ISBN: 0-89225-536-6

DEDICATION

To my husband, Milton, who loves being with people and has made our home welcome to all, giving the *gift of shelter*,

and to our children and their spouses, who have followed in his footsteps in their own homes.

To my mother, Dalphine Shannon, who has been an example of hospitality in giving the *gift of comfort* in caring for my brother and me and in caring for my dad in his illness, spending countless nights sitting at the side of his hospital bed without any thought for her own comfort.

To my husband's parents, Horace and Ruth Sewell, who exemplify the *gift of nourishment* as they grow, harvest, preserve and share vegetables from their garden, and in feeding so many of us at their table.

To my friend, Kay DeLay, who has a heart of compassion and gives to so many the *gift of companionship*.

To our ministers and their wives who are called on by all of us when we don't know who else to call, and so generously give the *gift of service*.

To the many among us who quietly go about doing good, sharing themselves and their possessions to ease the burdens of others, giving the *gift of benevolence*.

TABLE OF CONTENTS

Page

THE TOUGHEST TEST

As Christians, we give much thought to what it takes to become a child of God. We emphasize the need to read and study God's Word. We give careful attention to the proper mode of worship – in our singing, our praying, our communion, our teaching.

But Jesus gives us what may be the toughest test of all when He tells us about the final judgment. He spells out for us in no uncertain terms what will separate the saved from the lost – the sheep from the goats – and that is the way we treat others. Those who do not look after the needs of others will "go away into eternal punishment, but the righteous into eternal life" (Matthew 25:46).

Although we will not be able to eliminate poverty or relieve all suffering or even feed all who are hungry, we should be ready to follow the advice Paul gave to the Galatians: "So then, while we have opportunity, let us do good to all men, and especially to those who are of the household of the faith" (Galatians 6:10).

A KIND WORD

"Who gives himself with his alms
feeds three:
himself,
his hungering neighbor,
and Me."
James Russell Lowell

"I shall pass through this world but once.
Any good therefore that I can do or any kindness that I can
show to any human being, let me do it now. Let me not defer
or neglect it, for I shall not pass this way again."
Mahatma Gandhi

"Strew gladness on the paths of men –
You will not pass this way again."
Sam Walter Foss

CHAPTER 1

THEN SHALL
THE KING SAY ...

"Come, you who are blessed of My Father,
inherit the kingdom prepared for you from the
foundation of the world" (Matthew 25:34).

A few years ago I was asked to speak for a ladies day about hospitality. The suggested title was "Gift of Hospitality." As a second thought, the caller asked, "Or would you prefer it to be '*Gifts* of Hospitality'?" I chose the latter. I thought it would be interesting to think of several gifts we offer when we extend hospitality and gifts we receive as well.

As I began to work on the lesson, it was obvious that in extending hospitality, we give the *gift of nourishment* because most cases of hospitality involve sharing a meal. Even at church the word "fellowship" is often preceded by the words "finger food."

Often hospitality involves giving people a place to stay overnight. This home away from home is a *gift of shelter*.

The *gift of companionship* is inherent in getting together with others. And when we are looking after the needs of others, we provide the *gift of service*. Occasionally, we have an opportunity to provide hospitality to someone who is ill, giving the *gift of care and comfort*.

My lesson about hospitality was almost complete when I chanced to reread Matthew 25. In this passage, Jesus describes the final judgment where the King will separate the faithful from the unfaithful. I was stunned to see the lesson I was working on had been outlined some 2,000 years ago.

Although I had read Matthew 25 many times before, I had never connected it with hospitality. I realized that my understanding of hospitality was comparatively shallow. Hospitality is much more than getting acquainted, much more than a social exchange, much more even than fellowship. Hospitality, as described in Matthew 25, is meeting the needs of others, whatever those needs might be.

I realized my outline for my speech was incomplete without the *gift of benevolence*: "I was ... naked, and you clothed Me." Being hospitable demands that we help meet the material needs of others when it is within our power and opportunity to do so. Jesus, in explaining the judgment, said:

> But when the Son of Man comes in His glory, and all the angels with Him, then He will sit on His glorious throne. And all the nations will be gathered before Him; and He will separate them from one another, as the shepherd separates the sheep from the goats; and He will put the sheep on His right, and the goats on the left. Then the King will say to those on His right, "Come, you who are blessed of My Father, inherit the kingdom prepared for you from the foundation of the world. For I was hungry, and you gave Me something to eat; I was thirsty, and you gave Me drink; I was a stranger, and you invited Me in; naked, and you clothed Me; I was sick, and you visited Me; I was in prison, and you came to Me."
>
> Then the righteous will answer Him, saying, "Lord, when did we see You hungry, and feed You, or thirsty, and give You drink? And when did we see You a stranger, and invite You in, or naked, and clothe You? And when did we see You sick, or in prison, and come to You?" And the King will answer and say to them, "Truly I say to you, to the extent that you did it to one of these brothers of Mine, even the least of them, you did it to Me" (Matthew 25:31-40).

THE SIX GIFTS OF HOSPITALITY

Using these six situations as a model, we can identify six gifts that we may give to others when we offer our hospitality.

1. "For I was hungry, and you gave Me something to eat." We can give the gift of nourishment by preparing food for others.

2. "I was thirsty, and you gave Me drink." We can give the gift of service, whether by offering as little as a cup of cold water or offering any other service that might be needed.

3. "I was a stranger, and you invited Me in." Taking a person into our homes offers the gift of shelter.

4. "I was ... naked, and you clothed Me." We can give the gift of benevolence in providing for the material needs of others.

5. "I was sick, and you visited Me." The gift of comfort is often needed by the aged, by someone who has had surgery, by a mother with a new baby, by someone who is injured, or by someone who is ill.

6. "I was in prison, and you came to Me." People in actual prisons, or in virtual prisons of loneliness, may have all their physical needs met – food, clothing and shelter – but we can offer the gift of companionship to let them know they are not forgotten.

THE SIX BENEFITS OF HOSPITALITY

In giving, we also receive. Here are six benefits we receive from offering hospitality to others.

1. Friendship. When offering hospitality, you may develop friendships that last a lifetime. When we were a young married couple, our electricity once went off during a snowstorm, leaving us without heat. Our good friends shared their home with us. We made decorative candles, talked into the night, and then slept on pallets in their living room. That was more than 35 years ago, and we still talk about that evening with fondness.

2. Mentoring Children. Children model what they see. They learn from living in a home where having guests is as normal as any other routine. When they have homes of their own, it just seems natural for them to be hospitable also. Hospitality isn't the only thing children learn. They learn:

• To be polite. If they are never required to sit at the table and use good manners, how will they learn?

• To share. Children will learn to share their rooms, their toys, and their attention.

• To serve. Serving is giving of yourself and your time, as well as your resources.

• To meet people. The people who share your home may inspire your children. A friend related that when she was a child, a minister visiting her home talked about the importance of mission work to the Chinese people. She determined that one day she would go to China. She never forgot that dream, and now she is retired and happily involved in teaching the Bible to the people in China. You never know when a seed is being sown that will take root later.

3. Giving. Paul, quoting the words of Jesus, said, "It is more blessed to give than to receive" (Acts 20:35). In giving hospitality we have the opportunity to give back, repaying kindnesses done for us. "Give, and it will be given to you; good measure, pressed down, shaken together, running over, they will pour into your lap. For by your standard of measure it will be measured to you in return" (Luke 6:38).

4. Serving Others. Occasionally, we hear of someone who is experiencing some minor depression. A counselor may advise that person to go find someone who needs her help, for in giving of ourselves, we forget our own troubles and start looking outward in a more positive way. "For we are His workmanship, created in Christ Jesus for good works, which God prepared beforehand, that we should walk in them" (Ephesians 2:10).

5. God's Rewards. One of the benefits of extending hospitality to others is that we are rewarded by God for doing so. The Lord, through the prophet Malachi, chided the Israelites for bringing polluted food as an offering. He challenged them to: " 'Bring the whole tithe into the storehouse, so that there may be food in My house, and test Me now in this,' says the LORD of hosts, 'if I will not open for you the windows of heaven, and pour out for you a blessing until it overflows' " (Malachi 3:10). God will open for us the windows of heaven when we give our best to Him.

The much beloved African-American minister, Marshall Keeble, told about visiting philanthropist A.M. Burton and commenting to Burton that he just keeps "scooping out" to others. Burton replied, "Yes, but the Lord just has a bigger scoop." 6. A Good Name. One of the benefits of being hospitable is the good name it brings to the giver. Solomon said it well in his proverb, "A good name is to be more desired than great riches, Favor is better than silver and gold" (Proverbs 22:1). The value of a good name cannot be overstated. Trust is built on reputation.

In an article in the *Harvard University Gazette*, Alvin Powell writes that studies have determined the amount of trust placed in a good reputation can actually be measured. Researcher Richard Zeckhauser at the University of Michigan auctioned carefully matched items – five vintage Valentine postcards – from two sellers.

Powell writes, "One seller had a superb, long-established reputation, which on E-bay means many buyers had posted positive feedback after their transactions. The second set was auctioned by the same seller, but under a newly established identity with little or no track record.

"After selling 200 carefully matched pairs of postcards, the established identity had brought in 7.6 percent more, on average, from his transactions. 'It's a pretty fair rate of return for having a good reputation,' Zeckhauser said."

Although Christians are concerned with keeping a good name for reasons other than economics, it is interesting to note that a measurable amount of trust was placed in nothing more than a name with a good track record.

MOTIVATIONS FOR OFFERING HOSPITALITY

What should be the motivation for hospitality? Proper motivations for offering hospitality may include a love of God, a love for man, compassion and a desire to be of service. It also must include proper attitude. For example, 2 Corinthians 9:7 tells us to be joyful, Romans 12:9 says to be sincere, and 1 Peter 4:9 tells us to be hospitable without grumbling.

The story of the good Samaritan shows a proper motivation for hospitality. A traveler from Jerusalem to Jericho had fallen prey to thieves who stripped him, beat him, and left him for dead. "But a certain Samaritan, who was on a journey, came upon him; and when he saw him, he felt compassion" (Luke 10:33). Not only did the good Samaritan show compassion to the injured man, but he also seemed to help without grumbling.

The supreme motivation for true hospitality is a love for God and a love for people. "But whoever has the world's goods, and beholds his brother in need and closes his heart against him, how does the love of God abide in him?" (1 John 3:17).

WHEN HOSPITALITY IS NOT REALLY HOSPITALITY

Improper motivations for offering hospitality include the desires to manipulate people, to impress people, or to be seen of men (Matthew 6:2-4). In the case of Martha in Luke 10, she was more concerned about the physical part of hospitality than the spiritual aspect of it. Jesus said, "Martha, Martha, you are worried and bothered about so many things; but only a few things are necessary, really only one, for Mary has chosen the good part, which shall not be taken away from her" (Luke 10:41-42).

Hospitality is missing when it is insincere, given grudgingly or when the motive is self-serving. "Be hospitable to one another without complaint" (1 Peter 4:9).

"When therefore you give alms, do not sound a trumpet before you, as the hypocrites do in the synagogues and in the streets, that they may be honored by men. Truly I say to you, they have their reward in full" (Matthew 6:2).

In the Day of Judgment we will want to hear the King say,

> Come you who are blessed of my Father, inherit the kingdom prepared for you from the foundation of the world, for I was hungry and you shared your food with Me when I didn't have enough. I was thirsty and you served Me a cup of cold water. I was without a place to stay and you opened up your home for Me. I was in need of clothing and you purchased some for Me. I was sick

and you tenderly cared for Me. I was in prison, and you did not forget Me.

The only way we will be able to do these acts of hospitality for Jesus is to do them for those around us. Let us be ever mindful of opportunities to help others.

QUESTIONS

1. What are six deeds that will separate the saved from the lost in Jesus' description of the judgment?

2. What benefits do you receive when you offer hospitality to others?

3. The Bible tells us we were created for _____.

4. Name some proper and improper motivations for offering hospitality. Include some not listed in the lesson text.

5. What should be our attitude in extending hospitality?

SMALL GROUP DISCUSSION

1. Which gift or gifts do you feel most comfortable in giving? Why?

2. Which of these acts of hospitality is out of your comfort zone? What can you do to overcome this?

3. What is the reputation of your congregation in your community? Is it seen as a place to go when someone needs help?

A KIND WORD

How shall we tell an angel
From another guest?
How, from the common worldly herd,
One of the blest?

Hint of suppressed halo,
Rustle of hidden wings,
Wafture of heavenly frankincense, –
Which of these things?

The old Sphinx smiles so subtly:
"I give thee no golden rule, –
Yet would I warn thee, World: treat well
Whom thou call'st fool."
Gertrude Hall

---------- CHAPTER 2 ----------

DEFINING HOSPITALITY

"Do not neglect to show hospitality to strangers, for by this some have entertained angels without knowing it" (Hebrews 13:2).

What do you think when you hear the term "hospitality"? The hotel industry calls itself the "hospitality industry." No doubt this is an appropriate term because the larger hotels offer many elements of hospitality (albeit for a price): shelter for the night, amenities for the comfort of their guests, services of all kinds, and nourishment in their restaurants.

When we think of hospitality, most of us think about inviting someone we know into our homes for dinner. We think of the preparation necessary to make the house presentable, buying groceries, cooking the dinner, and setting the table.

Sometimes we may think we have to be somewhat like Martha Stewart to entertain. Everything has to be perfect. Our dinner parties must be lavishly decorated. Our house must be spotlessly clean and magazine perfect. We may feel reluctant to open our homes because we live more like Erma Bombeck, dealing with real-life stains on the carpet and the signs of wear and tear on our furniture.

One woman wrote about her experience in preparing for guests. She cleaned the house and placed a new set of matching towels in the bathroom. Fearing that her family would dirty them before the guests arrived, she pinned a note to one stating: "Do not touch these!" Imagine her dismay when she was cleaning up after the guests had gone and found the note still neatly attached to the unused towels.

Real hospitality is not dependent on silver service or matching towels, but on kindness, warm hearts, and a desire to meet the needs of others.

THE MEANING OF HOSPITALITY

Hospitality is a gift or rather a collection of gifts you give to others. Hospitality is a means of meeting the needs of others. We are told to be "rejoicing in hope, persevering in tribulation, devoted to prayer, contributing to the needs of the saints, practicing hospitality" (Romans 12:12-13).

We often think of hospitality as personal friends coming for a visit. Hospitality in the Bible includes so much more. It is not merely a reciprocal exchange of visits among friends – you invited us over for dinner, so we want to return the favor and invite you over. More often hospitality is a non-reciprocal meeting of the needs of another, especially the needs of strangers, the less fortunate, and even our enemies. It means doing for others who may never be in a position to repay us (Luke 14:12-14).

Notice those to whom hospitality is to be given:
- Strangers – Hebrews 13:2
- Enemies – Romans 12:20
- Poor, needy – James 1:27
- Sick, infirm – Matthew 25:36
- Imprisoned, lonely – Matthew 25:36
- Friends – 1 John 4:7
- Fellow Christians – Galatians 6:10
- Our own families – 1 Timothy 5:8

LET THE STRANGER IN

In the book *Hospitality: In the Spirit of Love*, Peggy Simpson states, "Meeting and getting to know strangers is not easy. It takes nerve to say, 'Why don't you come home with us for dinner?' "

Inviting people is never a problem in our family – my husband takes care of that! Other people collect stamps or antiques; he collects people. If there is a hymn that describes entertaining in our home, it might be "There's a Stranger at the Door."

If people are comfortable in our home, it is because my husband is comfortable with people. Whatever I may have learned about hospitality, I have learned from him and the many years of experience of living with him. Having guests in your home becomes easier the more you do it; that's why it is called practicing hospitality. No matter their profession or social status or what country they are from, people are basically the same.

• People like to eat, so have a good meal. It doesn't have to be fancy or expensive, just tasty and pleasing to the eyes – and enough of it.

• People are curious about how you live so show them through your house if they indicate an interest. They get to know you better when they see the way you live, what you collect, the pictures you display, the styles and colors you choose. Tell them about the quilt that is dear to you and why. Show them the picture of the new baby or grandbaby (but don't get out the videos and home movies).

• People enjoy talking about themselves, so ask questions that encourage them to share themselves with you. Often, the more we learn about others, the more common ground we find.

• People like to be treated special. If you know they like a certain food, try to have it for them. Once we had several guests for breakfast. Trying to be polite, I offered coffee, milk, juice or hot tea. One gentleman, whom we had just met, listened to the choices and then said, "I really wanted a cup of Ovaltine!" Of course he was teasing me, trying to ask for something I did not have, but the next year when he visited us again, you can be sure he found a jar of Ovaltine beside his cup, much to his delight!

• People want to feel comfortable, so don't constantly apologize for things – "I'm sorry our house needs painting" or "We don't have curtains for this room yet." Be assured, they have some of the same problems in their own houses.

You may need to explain some things, however. Once we had

invited a group of about 18 people to come to our house for breakfast (they were just passing through on their way home to Georgia after working in a vacation Bible school in New Mexico). We had recently moved into our new house so there were boxes still unpacked in every room. Also, on moving day, the builder had fallen through our kitchen ceiling. He wasn't hurt, but the ceiling had a huge hole in it that made a good topic of conversation!

• Your guests want you to feel comfortable too. Learn to take things in stride. Not every dish you cook will turn out perfect.

I remember many years ago inviting several preachers and their wives to our home for Sunday dinner. I had made the most beautiful apple dumplings. When I took them out of the oven, the aroma filled the room.

I set the glass casserole dish on top of the stove. As I was getting the dessert plates out, we heard a loud pop. Unfortunately, the stove burner was still hot, causing the dish to crack, and dumplings started sliding down the front of the oven onto the floor. I could have died! And to top it off, the guests came into the kitchen to see what had happened.

After they returned to their seats, I set out jams and jellies, and we served those with the buttered rolls for dessert. We had a good laugh, and, much to their credit, the other women shared stories of their own cooking disasters.

• People are the same the world over. I remember the first time we had a group of Russian students over for dinner. This was soon after the Iron Curtain was lifted, and we were just beginning to meet people from the former Soviet Union.

When I was younger, Americans had a certain amount of fear of Russians. I remember in junior high school a teacher showed us on a globe just how close our two countries were. Russia was just a few miles from Alaska.

As these students visited our home, I was curious to learn if they had also feared us. I asked, "Were you afraid of the United States?" One of the students answered, "Oh yes, I remember in school, one of my teachers held up a map and showed us just how close we were to your state of Alaska." We discovered a common bond, and the fear melted away.

We once hosted a lady from Romania. In fact, she was a princess. Our daughter Holly was in the first grade at the time and was very eager to meet this princess. She hurried home from school but was disappointed to learn that our guest was taking a nap in her bedroom. Walking down the hall I caught Holly lying on her stomach, trying to look under the door. When the princess awoke from her nap, I detected some disappointment in Holly. I guess she was expecting to see her royal highness with a tiara and an evening gown but was disappointed to find that the princess was just a little gray–haired grandmother.

Over the years, we have had guests from Australia, Poland, France, Spain and many other countries. They were much like us in many ways. It is delightful learning about their customs, and they, in turn, learn about ours.

• Although people are alike, they are also unique. Some you will thoroughly enjoy and will always feel close to. We were entertaining an attorney and his wife, whom I had never met. They were both very knowledgeable and polished people. But at the end of the meal, she did something that gave me an insight into her delightful sense of humor. She said, "Oh, that was so delicious, do you mind if I lick my plate?" Only after my initial shock did I notice the mischievous twinkle in her eye.

Be prepared, however, there may be some uncomfortable moments. I remember working hard to prepare a meal while caring for my preschool children. We had one gentleman for dinner whose main topic of conversation was how women don't know how to cook like they used to. "They all use instant potatoes and cake mixes instead of the real thing."

Can you guess two of the items on my menu? Instant potatoes and cake made from a mix. By the way he ate, though, I really don't think he ever knew.

• Don't forget, some of the most important people who will eat at your table are the members of your own family. I don't save my good china and silver for guests. I use it at least once a week for my husband and children – and even the grandchildren. I want them to know that they are valued as much as anyone, even as much as a little gray-haired princess from Romania.

THE MOST IMPORTANT COMMANDMENT

Hospitality in a broad sense is non-negotiable. For the Christian, it is a commandment: "You shall love your neighbor as yourself" (Matthew 22:39). It is not a matter of whether we wish to offer some form of hospitality but a vital part of our purpose in life.

Solomon spent much time in reflecting on his purpose in life and wrote, "I know that there is nothing better for them than to rejoice and to do good in one's lifetime" (Ecclesiastes 3:12). He also concluded that the wholeness of man is to fear God and keep His commandments.

Upon reflecting about the mission and purpose of man, Thomas P. Hardeman put into verse form what he believes to be the teaching of the Bible.

> For what the birth of the masses?
> Or why the lives of the few?
> To what run the paths of the greatest?
> Whither it leads, what they do?
> For what the breath that is given?
> Or whence the power to fly?
> For what all the glories of heaven?
> Is every answer a lie?
> Man born to die is a question,
> Ever and always to seek
> Not the mysteries of God high above him,
> But the mission of man who is weak.
> Is it pain? Is it joy? It is neither –
> Not regret nor false bliss can repay,
> But the good that he does to another
> Is the end of his life every day.

Paul stated it succinctly: "For we are His workmanship, created in Christ Jesus for good works" (Ephesians 2:10). This, then, is our purpose in life: to do good and to keep the commandments of God. Jesus illustrates for us what doing good is all about:

And one of the scribes came and heard them arguing, and recognizing that [Jesus] had answered them well, asked Him, "What commandment is the foremost of all?" Jesus answered, "The foremost is, 'Hear, O Israel! The Lord our God is one Lord; And you shall love the Lord your God with all your heart, and with all your soul, and with all your mind, and with all your strength.' The second is this, 'You shall love your neighbor as yourself.' There is no other commandment greater than these" (Mark 12:28-31).

Hospitality is indeed more than having friends in for a visit. Hospitality is about loving your neighbor.

QUESTIONS

1. How would you define hospitality?

2. How are people basically alike in their needs?

3. Hospitality in a biblical sense is often non-_____ and non-_____.

4. What are the two greatest commandments that hospitality fulfills (Mark 12:28-31)?

5. To whom should we offer hospitality?

SMALL GROUP DISCUSSION

1. What are some of the reasons that hinder you from offering hospitality more often?

2. How can a host and hostess make others feel welcome at their table?

A KIND WORD

"A hungry stomach cannot hear."
Jean de La Fontaine

"There's no sauce in the world like hunger."
Cervantes

"Better is a dish of vegetables where love is,
Than a fattened ox and hatred with it" (Proverbs 15:17).

"Sharing food with another human being
is an intimate act that
should not be indulged in lightly."
M.F.K. Fisher

CHAPTER 3

THE ROLE OF FOOD

THE GIFT OF NOURISHMENT, PART 1

"For I was hungry, and you gave Me something to eat."

It is hard to imagine extending hospitality for very long without food being involved. Our lives depend on physical nourishment, and the necessity for food cannot be ignored for many hours. Thus, the six gifts of hospitality in our study will, at some time or another, involve feeding people.

Food has played a role in many major events in biblical history. A piece of fruit was tempting enough to bring sin into the world. A mess of pottage was the price paid by Jacob for Esau's birthright. And by example, Jesus taught us the importance of giving food to people. When the crowd following Him became hungry, the disciples asked what to do about it. Jesus then performed a miracle to feed the multitude of people because He had compassion on them (Matthew 15:32).

Let's learn from others mentioned in the Scripture who were known for their hospitality in feeding people.

ANGELS WHO STAYED FOR DINNER

When Abraham was visited by angels, he invited them to eat with him. Notice the gifts of hospitality he extended (gifts, plural, is used here because often the gifts of hospitality are intertwined) and the attitude with which he entertained:

> Now the Lord appeared to him by the oaks of Mamre, while he was sitting at the tent door in the heat of the day. And when he lifted up his eyes and looked, behold, three men were standing opposite him; and when he saw them, he ran from the tent door to meet them, and bowed himself to the earth [*this hospitality was not grudgingly given*], and said, "My lord, if now I have found favor in your sight, please do not pass your servant by. Please let a little water be brought and wash your feet [*gift of service*], and rest [*gift of comfort*] yourselves under the tree [*gift of shelter from the heat of the day*]; and I will bring a piece of bread [*gift of nourishment*], that you may refresh yourselves; after that you may go on, since you have visited your servant." And they said, "So do, as you have said." So Abraham hurried into the tent to Sarah, and said, "Quickly, prepare three measures of fine flour, knead it, and make bread cakes."
>
> Abraham also ran to the herd, and took a tender and choice calf, and gave it to the servant; and he hurried to prepare it. And he took curds and milk and the calf which he had prepared, and placed it before them; and he was standing by them under the tree as they ate [*gift of companionship*] (Genesis 18:1-8).

Webster defines a servant as "one who exerts himself for the benefit of others." Abraham and Sarah truly served their guests.

The writer of Hebrews taught us, "Be not forgetful to entertain strangers: for thereby some have entertained angels unawares" (Hebrews 13:2 KJV).

BANQUET FOR THE BUILDERS
We remember the story of Nehemiah rebuilding the walls of Jerusalem, but we don't often mention the task he had daily of feeding all the workers.

And I also applied myself to the work on this wall; we did not buy any land, and all my servants were gathered there for the work. Moreover, there were at my table one hundred and fifty Jews and officials, besides those who came to us from the nations that were around us. Now that which was prepared for each day was one ox and six choice sheep, also birds were prepared for me; and once in ten days all sorts of wine were furnished in abundance. Yet for all this I did not demand the governor's food allowance, because the servitude was heavy on this people (Nehemiah 5:16-18).

GIVING FROM THE EMPTY CUPBOARD

After God had miraculously fed him by ravens, Elijah fled to a cave. The brook from which he needed water had dried up. God appeared to a widow in the village of Zarephath (1 Kings 17:8-16). She was hungry because of a famine in the land.

Then the word of the Lord came to him, saying, "Arise, go to Zarephath, which belongs to Sidon, and stay there; behold, I have commanded a widow there to provide for you."

So he arose and went to Zarephath, and when he came to the gate of the city, behold, a widow was there gathering sticks; and he called to her and said, "Please get me a little water in a jar, that I may drink." And as she was going to get it, he called to her and said, "Please bring me a piece of bread in your hand." But she said, "As the Lord your God lives, I have no bread, only a handful of flour in the bowl and a little oil in the jar; and behold, I am gathering a few sticks that I may go in and prepare for me and my son, that we may eat it and die."

Then Elijah said to her, "Do not fear; go, do as you have said, but make me a little bread cake from it first, and bring it out to me, and afterward you may make one for yourself and for your son. For thus says the Lord God of Israel, 'The bowl of flour shall not be exhausted,

nor shall the jar of oil be empty, until the day that the
Lord sends rain on the face of the earth.'"

So she went and did according to the word of Elijah,
and she and he and her household ate for many days.
The bowl of flour was not exhausted nor did the jar of
oil become empty, according to the word of the Lord
which He spoke through Elijah.

PEACE MEAL

Abigail, a beautiful woman of good understanding, knew the
power of good food in easing tensions between adversaries. Her
husband, Nabal, on the other hand, is described as harsh and evil.

On one occasion, King David's men were in the wilderness and
in need of food. David heard that Nabal was shearing his sheep
so David sent out 10 young men with these instructions:

> Go up to Carmel, visit Nabal and greet him in my
> name; and thus you shall say, "Have a long life, peace
> be to you, and peace be to your house, and peace be
> to all that you have.
>
> "And now I have heard that you have shearers; now
> your shepherds have been with us and we have not in-
> sulted them, nor have they missed anything all the days
> they were in Carmel.
>
> "Ask your young men and they will tell you. There-
> fore let my young men find favor in your eyes, for we
> have come on a festive day. Please give whatever you
> find at hand to your servants and to your son David"
> (1 Samuel 25:5-8).

It was a reasonable request of someone who had plenty and
whose own shearers had been treated well by David when they
were in a similar situation. But Nabal was not a reasonable man.
He responded, "Who is David? And who is the son of Jesse? There
are many servants today who are each breaking away from his
master" (1 Samuel 25:10).

Notice the rest of his statement: "Shall I then take my bread and
my water and my meat that I have slaughtered for my shearers, and

give it to men whose origin I do not know?" (1 Samuel 25:11). One of the young men told Abigail how Nabal had treated David's men, although they themselves had been well treated when they had been in David's territory. They entreated her to consider what to do because this action would surely cause trouble for all of them and Nabal was such a worthless man they couldn't talk to him.

So Abigail hurriedly took 200 loaves, two bottles of wine, five sheep ready dressed, five measures of parched corn, 100 clusters of raisins, and 200 cakes of figs, and laid them on the donkeys. She told her servants to go on before her and she would follow. She left without informing Nabal of her plans.

In the meantime, David's men reported how rudely they had been treated. David reacted with war in his eyes and ordered 400 of his men to get their swords and follow him.

And so it was, as Abigail was coming down the hill, she bravely met David and his 400 sword-wielding men. She met him in humility, bowing herself to the ground at his feet. After making an impassioned plea for him not to take vengeance, but to accept her offering, David relented and said, "Blessed be the Lord God of Israel, who sent you this day to meet me, and blessed be your discernment, and blessed be you, who have kept me this day from bloodshed, and from avenging myself by my own hand" (1 Samuel 25:32-33).

Thus with her hospitality she turned away bloodshed and made up for the rudeness of her husband Nabal in his refusal to provide hospitality and food to his visitors.

Ten days later Nabal was struck dead, and David sent for Abigail to be his wife (1 Samuel 25:2-42).

FEEDING FOES

Elisha fed his enemies in an unusual and amusing circumstance. The military strategy of the king of Aram (Syria, KJV) had been upset several times as Elisha repeatedly conveyed the king's plans to the king of Israel. The Aramean king ordered his troops to seize Elisha, but Elisha cleverly led the Aramean troops straight into enemy territory in the city of Samaria.

When the king of Israel saw them, he asked Elisha, " 'My father, shall I kill them?' Elisha's surprising answer was, 'You shall not kill them. Would you kill those you have taken captive with your sword and with your bow? Set bread and water before them, that they may eat and drink and go to their master' " (2 Kings 6:22). The king of Israel complied and ordered a huge meal to be prepared for this enemy army. When the surprised but grateful troops finished eating, he let them go. The result? "And the marauding bands of Arameans did not come again into the land of Israel" (2 Kings 6:23).

When we lived in another city, the school where my husband served as an administrator joined the property of a rather unhappy woman. She complained about everything concerning the school. If a ball from a baseball game rolled into her yard, she was furious. And woe to the person who might be caught trespassing!

She happened also to be a member of the congregation we were attending. After bending my husband's ear one too many times, he decided to invite her to Sunday dinner at our house. She seemed rather surprised but accepted his invitation.

We had a nice visit, but about halfway through the meal she looked up and, shaking her fork, said, "I know what you're doing! You're heaping coals of fire on my head!"

Paul writes in Romans 12:19-20:

> Never take your own revenge, beloved, but leave room for the wrath of God, for it is written, "Vengeance is mine, I will repay," says the Lord.
>
> "But if your enemy is hungry, feed him, and if he is thirsty, give him a drink; for in so doing you will heap burning coals upon his head."

HOSPITALITY IN THE MIDST OF TURMOIL

Sometimes the breaking of bread together in a tense situation can have a calming effect. As a prisoner for the "crime" of preaching, Paul was being delivered by ship to Italy. After several days at sea, the winds increased, making their passage dangerous.

The ship was constantly tossed about by the storm. The crew

began throwing cargo overboard and the next day resorted to throwing the ship's tackle over the side. After two weeks in the ship, still battling the storm, Paul encouraged his captors. He told them God had sent an angel to him saying that none of them would perish. Paul also encouraged the men to take time to eat, for this was the 14th day that they had been watching the storm and neglecting to eat.

In the midst of the howling winds and tossing waves, Paul took bread, gave thanks to God in the presence of all, broke it and began to eat. They were encouraged – all 276 persons – and they themselves took food and ate. Here was Paul, a prisoner, offering hospitality in the worst of circumstances (Acts 27).

In a later chapter, we will observe the events that took place after this storm and see Paul's hospitality being repaid in an equally dramatic fashion.

NOURISHING OUR SPIRITS

We nourish not only our bodies with food but also our spirits. Most celebrations involve food: birthday cakes, Thanksgiving turkey and dressing, picnics on the Fourth of July.

Homecomings also are associated with food. When the prodigal son came home, his father killed the fatted calf and had a great feast prepared.

Sitting around a table can nourish our spirits as well as our bodies. I remember dinners at my grandparents' homes. The custom then was for the women – my grandmother, my mother and my aunts – to feed the men first. After the men's plates had been cleared away, the men retired to the living room to sit by the fire in wintertime or under the shade trees in summer. Then the women and children would sit down to eat and relax before beginning the task of washing, drying and putting away the dishes.

It seems more the custom now to try to feed everyone at the same time, either served at the table or by buffet. I sometimes wish for that unhurried time of sharing among the women about things that were common among them and the passing of traditions from one generation to the next.

Jan des Bouvrie Opsij of the Netherlands expressed her thoughts about the dynamics of sitting together at a table to eat:

> My philosophy is that true intimacy and romance always flourish at tables, not on sofas. At the table you have the best eye contact, and that's what it's all about. People push their empty plates to one side and linger longer and longer at the table. Once, people used to move from the dining table to the couch. That was a disaster because all the intimacy they had built up disappeared and they had to start all over. A table is the most beautiful piece of furniture there is.

Jacqueline Kennedy, the gracious hostess of the White House during her husband's presidency, knew the value of intimate table seating. Previous to their tenure, all official dinners had tables arranged in long formal U-shaped or E-shaped configurations. Mrs. Kennedy changed this to round tables, seating only eight people at each, to encourage conversation among her guests.

The food we provide does not need to be elaborate to be appreciated. One summer when my husband and I were vacationing in New York state, we stopped to visit Hyde Park and toured Springwood, the home of President Franklin Delano and Eleanor Roosevelt. The guide related a story about the time in 1939 when the Roosevelts were honored with a visit from the king and queen of England, George VI and Elizabeth. FDR planned a picnic for their guests on the grounds of Val-Kill, Eleanor's stone cottage.

FDR's mother, Sara, was horrified to know that he intended to serve them common hot dogs. He persisted. The king and queen were puzzled at the strange-looking sandwich and courteously informed their host that there seemed to be no silverware with which to eat it. Amused, FDR demonstrated how to pick it up with his hands and proceeded to eat. They were delighted! It was one of the highlights of their visit. Our guide told us that as long as she lived, Elizabeth, by then known as the Queen Mother, remembered the picnic of hot dogs at Val-Kill.

Incidentally, on the same visit from the king and queen to the Roosevelts' mansion, they were attending a more formal meal in the dining room. A small sideboard was called into duty to help accommodate extra guests in addition to the large dining table. Unfortunately, the small table had one rather wobbly leg, which they had neglected to repair. Just as the dinner was to begin, the leg collapsed, sending china, crystal and silver crashing to the floor. So ladies, it happens in the best of families!

Hospitality involves giving the gift of nourishment. When eating together, we nourish our bodies and our friendships. Mealtimes should be made as pleasant and unhurried as possible, which, in this day, is certainly a challenge.

QUESTIONS

1. What was Jesus' motivation for performing a miracle to feed a multitude of people?

2. What gifts of hospitality did Abraham offer his visitors?

3. How did the widow of Zarephath show hospitality to Elijah?

4. How did Nabal show his selfishness and lack of hospitality?

5. How did Paul use the gift of nourishment to encourage his fellow shipmates?

SMALL GROUP DISCUSSION

1. Have you ever used hospitality as an opportunity to be a peacemaker?

2. What pleasant memories do you have that are associated with mealtimes?

3. In your congregation, what avenues are available to help feed those who are truly hungry?

A KIND WORD

"Here is bread, which strengthens man's
heart, and therefore called the staff of life."
Matthew Henry

"Christianity is one beggar telling another beggar
where he found bread."
D. T. Niles

"It was a common saying among the Puritans,
'Brown bread and the Gospel is good fare.' "
Matthew Henry

"Bread is the king of the table and all else is merely
the court that surrounds the king."
Louis Bromfield

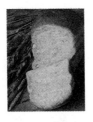

CHAPTER 4

OUR DAILY BREAD

THE GIFT OF NOURISHMENT, PART 2

"Give us this day our daily bread."

In thinking about the gift of nourishment and feeding people, one food stands out in biblical literature, and that is bread. References to bread keep popping up like toast out of a toaster. The first reference to bread occurs in Genesis, when God told Adam, "By the sweat of your face You shall eat bread, Till you return to the ground, Because from it you were taken; For you are dust, And to dust you shall return" (Genesis 3:19).

Jesus referred to Himself as the "bread of life" (John 6:35). He was born in Bethlehem, otherwise known as "the house of bread."

Bread is so important to us that we not only refer to the actual food by that name, but occasionally we also use it to refer to all food in general. Bread is also used to represent the Word of God in feeding our spiritual hunger. "Jesus said to them, 'I am the bread of life; he who comes to Me shall not hunger, and he who believes in Me shall never thirst' " (John 6:35).

MANNA, WHAT IS IT?

When the Israelites were being delivered from Egyptian bondage, they were instructed to take with them unleavened bread.

Leaving Egypt in haste, the Israelites (600,000, not counting the children) carried with them their kneading bowls and unleavened dough. This mass exodus was later celebrated each year as the Feast of Unleavened Bread.

As the Israelites wandered in the wilderness, they began to complain about the shortage of food. They wished they had died in Egypt "when we sat by the pots of meat, when we ate bread to the full" (Exodus 16:3). God then said, "I will rain bread from heaven for you." This bread was in a fine, flake-like form that covered the ground each morning. The Israelites named it manna, because they asked, "What is it?"

Jesus referred to this bread from heaven when He said:

> I am the bread of life. Your fathers ate the manna in the wilderness, and they died. This is the bread which comes down out of heaven, so that one may eat of it and not die. I am the living bread that came down out of heaven; if anyone eats of this bread, he shall live forever; and the bread also which I shall give for the life of the world is My flesh (John 6:48-51).

BREAD IN THE TABERNACLE

When the tabernacle was built, God instructed that three things be placed in the ark of the covenant: the tablets of the commandments, Aaron's rod that budded, and bread – "a golden jar holding the manna" (Hebrews 9:4). These three symbols served as a reminder of God's law, God's authority and God's providence.

Bread was also one of the three items featured in the holy place of the tabernacle: the golden candlesticks, the altar of incense and the table of shewbread or bread of the Presence. "Then you shall take fine flour and bake twelve cakes with it; two-tenths of an ephah shall be in each cake. And you shall set them in two rows, six to a row, on the pure gold table before the Lord" (Leviticus 24:5-6). This bread was to be presented to the Lord and later consumed by Aaron and his sons.

BREAD – THE SUBJECT OF DREAMS

Bread was the subject of significant dreams. The chief baker had a dream about three baskets of bread on his head. After telling his dream to Joseph, he learned the unpleasant interpretation that he had only three days left to live (Genesis 40:16-19).

Gideon received a message from God through a dream about bread. A man was overheard relating to a friend, "Behold, I had a dream; a loaf of barley bread was tumbling into the camp of Midian, and it came to the tent and struck it so that it fell, and turned it upside down so that the tent lay flat."

When the friend heard this dream, he said, "This is nothing less than the sword of Gideon the son of Joash, a man of Israel; God has given Midian and all the camp into his hand." When Gideon overheard this, he knew that he would be successful in overtaking Midian (Judges 7:13-14).

BREAD – A TEMPTATION

As we traveled by bus through the hills around the city of Jerusalem, our guide pointed out the many smooth stones dotting the hillsides. These had the appearance of the rounded, delicately browned loaves of bread we had seen earlier in shops along the streets in the city. We were reminded of Satan's temptation of Jesus when Jesus had been fasting for more than a month.

At His most vulnerable moment, Satan pointed out those smooth brown stones, looking so much like newly baked loaves that one could almost smell the aroma, and said, "If You are the Son of God, command that these stones become bread" (Matthew 4:3).

Jesus gave us a powerful example of withstanding temptation by refusing to give in, even in a time of great desire. He quoted the scripture, "It is written, 'Man shall not live on bread alone, but on every word that proceeds out of the mouth of God'" (Matthew 4:4).

BREAD – A MEMORIAL

In teaching His disciples to pray, the only physical blessing Jesus requested was bread: "Give us this day our daily bread" (Matthew 6:11). Bread is often used to represent all food for our bodies, as well as the familiar loaf made of flour, shortening and milk. Bread is also used in a spiritual sense. Jesus said, "I am the bread of life" (John 6:48). Breaking bread together on the first day of the week is a memorial to Him.

In our country and around the world, people have erected large memorials to honor distinguished persons. The Washington Monument reminds us of the first president of the United States. The Lincoln Memorial, with its massive seated statue of Abraham Lincoln, pays tribute to him and to his accomplishments. Universities, bridges and highways around the country bear the names of people who have made contributions to society. Almost every major city in the United States has a Martin Luther King Boulevard to honor the civil rights leader. All around the world elaborate buildings, tombs or statues memorialize people.

In contrast, Jesus chose a simple act of hospitality – the breaking of bread – to serve as a remembrance of Himself. "And when He had taken some bread and given thanks, He broke it, and gave it to them, saying, 'This is My body which is given for you; do this in remembrance of Me'" (Luke 22:19).

Each week, Christians around the world pause for quiet meditation and reflection on the sacrifice of Jesus while breaking bread in the company of others of "like precious faith." This simple act of breaking bread together serves as a bond and an agreement among the participants much like sharing a meal together.

This practice is like the one we read about in Acts 2 after Peter had so powerfully preached the first gospel sermon. "So then, those who had received his word were baptized; and there were added that day about three thousand souls. And they were continually devoting themselves to the apostles' teaching and to fellowship, to the breaking of bread and to prayer" (Acts 2:41-42).

BREAKING BREAD TOGETHER

Sharing a meal with someone usually signifies some measure of companionship with the person. David wrote, "Do not incline my heart to any evil thing, to practice deeds of wickedness With men who do iniquity; And do not let me eat of their delicacies" (Psalm 141:4).

The word "companion" comes from two Latin words, "*com*"

meaning "with" and *"panion"* meaning "bread." The word "companion" literally means to be "with bread."

The Pharisees and scribes were critical of Jesus when they saw Him eating with the tax collectors and sinners who were coming to hear Him. "Why is He eating and drinking with tax-gatherers and sinners?" Jesus said to them, "It is not those who are healthy who need a physician, but those who are sick; I did not come to call the righteous, but sinners" (Mark 2:17).

Interestingly, it was an act of hospitality, the breaking of bread, that caused Jesus' disciples to recognize Him. After His death and resurrection, Jesus appeared to two of His followers as they walked along the road to Emmaus. He approached them as they talked, and they began to tell Him all about the death of Jesus the Nazarene, "who was a prophet mighty in deed and word in the sight of God and all the people, and how the chief priests and our rulers delivered Him up to the sentence of death, and crucified Him" (Luke 24:19-20).

Jesus, still unrecognized by them, was invited to stay with them because it was getting late. As Jesus came to the table, He took the bread and blessed it and after breaking it He began giving it to them. Their eyes were opened, and they recognized Him. "He was recognized by them in the breaking of the bread" (Luke 24:35).

THE IMPORTANCE OF BREAD

It is difficult for us to imagine the importance of bread to the people in the Middle East. Elsie Huffard, who served for 13 years as a missionary with her husband in Israel, recalls this incident, which may help us understand: Upon finding some bread that had molded, Elsie threw it in the garbage can. Her houseboy, on seeing this, scolded her, saying, "You must not throw away bread." Elsie explained to him that it was moldy and therefore not fit to be eaten. His answer was that it must be put out for the birds to eat, and therefore not wasted.

The making of bread was so vital to the Hebrew people that even the Mosaical Law stipulated that one could not take a millstone, or even the upper half of a millstone, as collateral: "No one shall take a handmill or an upper millstone in pledge, for he would be taking a life in pledge" (Deuteronomy 24:6). To take away one's millstone was to take away his means of grinding grain and making bread.

THE IMPORTANCE OF INGREDIENTS

The ingredients of bread are often referred to in Scripture in symbolic ways:

• Wheat. Ground into flour, wheat was a common ingredient in bread. Jesus used wheat in a parable to represent good as opposed to tares, or weeds, which represented evil (Matthew 13:24-30).

• Leaven. "He spoke another parable to them, 'The kingdom of heaven is like leaven, which a woman took, and hid in three pecks of meal, until it was all leavened'" (Matthew 13:33).

"Beware of the leaven of the Pharisees, which is hypocrisy" (Luke 12:1).

"Your boasting is not good. Do you not know that a little leaven leavens the whole lump of dough?" (1 Corinthians 5:6).

• Salt. "You are the salt of the earth; but if the salt has become tasteless, how will it be made salty again? It is good for nothing anymore, except to be thrown out and trampled under foot by men" (Matthew 5:13).

"Let your speech always be with grace, seasoned, as it were, with salt, so that you may know how you should respond to each person" (Colossians 4:6).

• Milk. "Like newborn babes, long for the pure milk of the word, that by it you may grow in respect to salvation" (1 Peter 2:2).

"For everyone who partakes only of milk is not accustomed to the word of righteousness, for he is a babe" (Hebrews 5:13).

• Oil. Oil is precious not only for its use as a food, but also as fuel: "but the prudent took oil in flasks along with their lamps" (Matthew 25:4). Oil was valued for its medicinal uses. The Samaritan "came to him, and bandaged up his wounds, pouring oil and wine on them" (Luke 10:34). And oil was used for anointing: "Thou hast anointed my head with oil; My cup overflows" (Psalm 23:5).

PREPARING THE LOAF

Several years ago, the women in a congregation took turns preparing the unleavened bread for communion; perhaps some still do. However, most now use commercially prepared unleavened bread for the sake of convenience.

The following recipe appeared in an issue of the *Gospel Advocate* many years ago and may be of historical interest to those who have rendered this service of love and for all other Christian women, as well.

Recipe for Unleavened Bread

¾ cup of plain flour
2 level tablespoons of shortening
3½ tablespoons of water, or sufficient amount to make dough just moist enough to hold together.

Cut in the shortening with two knives or pastry blender, leaving shortening in pieces about the size of small peas. Add the water, a tablespoon at a time, mixing with a fork. Roll thin on lightly floured board. Cut in desired sizes and mark each loaf in small checks with a dull knife. Bake in oven at about 425 degrees. If blisters form while baking, press down with cloth or paper napkin. This makes about eight 3½- x 3½-inch loaves.

The following was first published in the *Gospel Advocate* in 1886 and was signed "Rachel." She described making the bread for communion, and added:

I always beat the dough a while with the rolling pin, and while doing so, this scripture invariably comes to my mind: "He was wounded for our transgressions, he was bruised for our iniquities." As I take the knife and make stripes across it, I am always reminded of "with His stripes we are healed." (Signed) Rachel

Jesus said of Himself, "I am the bread of life: he that comes to Me shall not hunger, and he who believes in Me shall never thirst" (John 6:35).

"The Lord Jesus in the night in which He was betrayed took bread; and when He had given thanks, He broke it, and said, 'This is My body, which is for you; do this in remembrance of Me'" (1 Corinthians 11:23-24).

Bread is our daily reminder of God's providence and His hospitality toward us and our weekly reminder of the sacrifice of Jesus.

QUESTIONS

1. What is the significance of unleavened bread?

2. What memorial reminds us of Jesus?

3. In addition to food, what does bread represent?

4. What act of worship is also an act of hospitality with others?

5. After Jesus' resurrection, what was He doing when His followers finally realized who He was?

SMALL GROUP DISCUSSION

1. When you partake of the communion bread, what thoughts cross your mind? What helps you keep your mind on the communion?

2. When has "breaking bread" with a group been particularly meaningful to you?

A KIND WORD

No service in itself is small,
None great, though earth it fill,
But that is small that seeks its own,
And great that seeks God's will.
Anonymous

"Serve the Lord with gladness" (Psalm 100:2).

"The service we render others
is the rent we pay for our room on this earth."
Wilfred Grenfell

CHAPTER 5

A CUP OF COLD WATER

THE GIFT OF SERVICE

"I was thirsty, and you gave Me drink."

A servant is first of all one who is under submission to another. For Christians, this means submission to God first, and then submission to one another. Submission is a difficult task for some. In Florence, Ala., where I grew up, there is a historical marker outside the city cemetery. It marks the burial place for "Mountain" Tom Clark, who boasted "no one will ever run over me!" After he confessed to at least 19 murders, the outraged citizens had him hanged and buried under the street outside the cemetery. Since 1872, every traveler going through Florence on U.S. Highway 72 has run over Tom Clark, bringing his boast to no avail.

Being a servant does not mean that you are allowing others to run over you. It is a voluntary submission to meet the needs of others. Jesus had the attitude of a servant. "For even the Son of Man did not come to be served, but to serve, and to give His life a ransom for many" (Mark 10:45).

REBEKAH'S GIFT OF SERVICE

It was a comfortable routine, going to the well and drawing water for the family and any one else who might need a drink of water. No doubt it had become second nature to her. Filling the big pots with fresh, cold well water, lifting them on her shoulder and returning to her tent, Bethuel's daughter Rebekah was accustomed to serving others.

But on this day, her hospitable nature would change the course of her life. Abraham's servant had been commissioned by his master to find a wife for his son Isaac.

To be certain he found the right wife for Isaac, he prayed,

> Behold, I am standing by the spring, and the daughters of the men of the city are coming out to draw water; now may it be that the girl to whom I say, "Please let down your jar so that I may drink," and who answers, "Drink, and I will water your camels also"; – may she be the one whom Thou hast appointed for Thy servant Isaac; and by this I shall know that Thou hast shown lovingkindness to my master (Genesis 24:13-14).

Before he had finished speaking, Rebekah appeared with a jar on her shoulder. She hurriedly went down to the spring, filled her jar and came back up. The servant ran to her and said, "Please let me drink a little water from your jar."

This beautiful girl responded, "Drink, my Lord." When she had finished giving him a drink, the servant's pulse must have quickened a bit when she continued, "I will draw also for your camels until they have finished drinking." Here was the sign for which he had prayed!

She ran to draw water for him and his camels, showing her eagerness to serve. And this was no small task, for a camel drinks a lot of water, and he had brought, not one camel, but 10!

Pushing his luck a bit, he said, "Whose daughter are you? Please tell me, is there room for us to lodge in your father's house?"

"And she said to him, 'I am the daughter of Bethuel, the son of Milcah, whom she bore to Nahor. We have plenty of both straw and feed, and room to lodge in.'"

Thus Rebekah gave even more than the servant had prayed for – not only water for himself and his camels, but also straw, feed and shelter for the night.

"FOR I HAVE GIVEN YOU AN EXAMPLE ..."

Jesus taught that hospitality can be as simple as offering a cup of cold water to someone: "And whoever in the name of a disciple gives to one of these little ones even a cup of cold water to drink, truly I say to you, he shall not lose his reward" (Matthew 10:42).

Near the end of Jesus' earthly life, He knew He was about to leave His disciples to return to heaven. Just as mothers give last-minute instructions before leaving their children, Jesus had another important instruction to give to His spiritual children. Rising from the supper table, He laid aside His outer clothing and wrapped Himself in a towel. Pouring water into a basin, He knelt down and began to wash the disciples' feet and to wipe them with the towel.

Peter looked on incredulously and asked, "Lord, do You wash my feet?" (John 13:6). After all, was that the job of a lord, to perform such a lowly service to those under his lordship? Wasn't it supposed to be the other way around?

Jesus explained that Peter might not understand now, but it would become clear to him later. But Peter protested, "Never shall You wash my feet!" Jesus said, "If I do not wash you, you have no part with Me." Then Peter, having it explained to him in this way, said, "Lord, not my feet only, but also my hands and my head."

And so when He had washed their feet, and taken His garments, and reclined at the table again, He said to them, "Do you know what I have done to you? You call Me Teacher and Lord; and you are right, for so I am. If I then, the Lord and the Teacher, washed your feet, you also ought to wash one another's feet.

"For I gave you an example that you also should do as I did to you. Truly, truly, I say to you, a slave is not greater than his master; neither is one who is sent greater than the one who sent him. If you know these things, you are blessed if you do them" (John 13:12-17).

Peter must have learned this lesson well, for later he wrote, "Be hospitable to one another without complaint. As each one has received a special gift, employ it in serving one another, as good stewards of the manifold grace of God" (1 Peter 4:9-10).

SHE AROSE AND MINISTERED

Peter's mother-in-law knew well the art of serving others. In fact, it makes me smile to read about her. She was in bed with a fever when Jesus came to the house. He merely touched her hand and the fever left her. She could have continued lying there, telling her family, "Oh, you just wouldn't believe how sick I've been," and enjoyed their continued concern. Instead, when the fever left her and she was no longer ill, she got up – probably washed her hands, tied on a clean apron, and headed for the kitchen. Matthew records that "the fever left her; and she arose, and waited on Him" (Matthew 8:14-15). She had the heart of a servant.

SERVICE TO OTHERS EQUALS MATURITY

Maturity and service go hand in hand. When a baby is born, he is totally self-centered. He cries when he needs to be fed. He demands to have a dry diaper. Everyone must adapt to his needs. As he matures, he begins to communicate his needs in a less demanding way and begins to take care of some of those needs himself, feeding himself little bites of food.

As that little child continues to mature, he will begin to help other family members. As a mature adult, he will consider his own needs and accept the responsibility for those who are less mature than himself. That's the way we mature physically.

Similarly, we mature in a spiritual way when we become less self-centered and more willing to put others first. Jesus said, "[W]hoever wishes to become great among you shall be your servant" (Matthew 20:26).

ACTS OF SERVICE TODAY

Although customs have changed through the years and across cultural lines, men and women still show hospitality through their acts of service. Young women assist by keeping one another's children. Ladies of the congregation take food to people who are ill. Young men offer their strength on moving day to assist families moving into the community. Young people get together to rake yards for the elderly. The people who agree to teach Bible classes are offering a service. The opportunities are all around us.

Paul wrote to the Galatians: "For you were called to freedom, brethren; only do not turn your freedom into an opportunity for the flesh, but through love serve one another. For the whole Law is fulfilled in one word, in the statement, 'You shall love your neighbor as yourself' " (Galatians 5:13-14).

QUESTIONS

1. What did Peter's mother-in-law do as soon as she was healed of her fever?

2. Who gave us an example of service with a basin of water?

3. What was the great compliment Jesus gave to the woman at Simon's house?

4. Jesus taught us that hospitality is serving the needs of others and can be as simple as offering a cup of _____ _____.

5. How are we to offer hospitality to one another?

6. How was Rebekah chosen as Isaac's wife?

7. Rebekah provided what elements of hospitality to Abraham's servant?

SMALL GROUP DISCUSSION

1. Can you think of a time when someone served you in a special way? What was that service?

2. Among your acquaintances, name three people who may need a gift of your services this week. What can you do for them?

3. How are service to others and maturity related?

A KIND WORD

"Home was quite a place,
when people stayed there."
E.B. White

"To invite a person into your home is to take charge
of his happiness for as long as he is under your roof."
A. Brillat Savarin

"If you would have guests merry with cheer,
Be so yourself, ... or at least appear."
From Poor Richard's Almanac

I have found such joy in simple things;
A plain clean room, a nut-brown loaf of bread,
A cup of milk, a kettle as it sings,
The shelter of a roof above my head,
And in a leaf-laced square along a floor,
Where yellow sunlight glimmers through a door.

I have found such joy in things that fill
My quiet days: a curtain's blowing grace,
A potted plant upon my windowsill,
A rose fresh-cut and placed within a vase;
A table cleared, a lamp beside a chair,
And books I long have loved beside me there.
Grace Noll Crowell

"Be hospitable to one another without complaint" (1 Peter 4:9).

— CHAPTER 6 —

WHEN THERE IS NO ROOM IN THE INN

THE GIFT OF SHELTER

"I was a stranger, and you invited Me in."

Home – what a sweet word! What woman among us has not played house as a child! I remember happy summer afternoons of playing "house" with my friends and cousins at my granddaddy's home. Arranging several cardboard boxes to serve as furniture, one box with four circles drawn on top became a stove. Discarded bottles from his Watkins' route became the spice bottles for the kitchen. Twigs served as room dividers.

In our childish minds, all people had houses with walls and a roof, and everyone's home had furniture. It simply was not in our imaginations that there were people without homes. Even now, as an adult, I find I take for granted the fact that I have shelter to live in.

TAKING HOME WITH YOU

A few years ago, we visited Africa and saw firsthand the huts made of twigs, mud and cow dung that some people call home. Entering the hut, we were shown the kitchen, which consisted of large rocks arranged in a circle to contain a fire for cooking. Directly above was a hole in the top of the hut for the smoke to escape. This was also the bedroom, because nearby was a puddle of fabric that served as a bed. A small calf being weaned from its mother occupied an adjacent room. This was home for them.

In 2009, the Three Gorges Dam along the Yangtze River in China will be completed. Many homes along the river will be destroyed, and some 1.13 million people will be displaced. An unusual response to this is taking place. The people along the river are moving to higher ground in anticipation of the completion of the dam. Many of the Chinese people have already begun dismantling their houses, salvaging as much as they can, particularly the rooftops. This way they can continue to live, literally and symbolically, under the same roof as before.

HOSPITALITY DOES NOT DEPEND ON THE HOUSE

Houses come in different shapes and styles. However, hospitality does not depend on the house but on the desire to share. *Unger's Bible Dictionary* describes hospitality in the Oriental lands as:

> ... a sacred duty to receive, feed, lodge and protect any traveler who might stop at the door. The stranger was treated as a guest, and men who had thus eaten together were bound to each other by the strongest ties of friendship.
>
> The present practice of the Arabs is the nearest approach to the ancient Hebrew hospitality. A traveler may sit at the door of a perfect stranger and smoke his pipe until the master welcomes him with an evening meal, and may tarry a limited number of days without inquiry as to his purposes, and depart with a simple "God be with you" as his only compensation. As the Hebrews became more numerous, inns were provided but these did not entirely supersede home hospitality.

Hospitality is translated from the Greek word "*philoxenia*," which is a combination of the words "*philo*" and "*xenia*." *Philo* means love, *xenia* means lodging, *xenos* is translated stranger or host, and *xenizo* is defined as "to lodge or entertain as a guest." Thus to be hospitable, one loves hosting or lodging strangers as guests.

God instructed the Israelites, "When a stranger resides with you in your land, you shall not do him wrong. The stranger who resides with you shall be to you as the native among you, and you shall love him as yourself; for you were aliens in the land of Egypt: I am the Lord your God" (Leviticus 19:33-34).

ADDING ON A PROPHET'S ROOM

One of the most beautiful examples of hospitality is that of a Shunammite woman, recorded in the book of 2 Kings:

> Now there came a day when Elisha passed over to Shunem, where there was a prominent woman, and she persuaded him to eat food. And so it was, as often as he passed by, he turned in there to eat food. And she said to her husband, "Behold now, I perceive that this is a holy man of God passing by us continually. Please, let us make a little walled upper chamber and let us set a bed for him there, and a table and a chair and a lampstand; and it shall be, when he comes to us, that he can turn in there" (2 Kings 4:8-10).

When Elisha offered to repay her by speaking on her behalf to the king or to the captain of the army, she declined, showing that she had done this with no thought of personal gain or repayment of any kind. Nor was it because she was lonely and in need of company, for she provided him a private place in which to rest.

How did she demonstrate hospitality? She was perceptive of his needs. She fed him. She gave him privacy and a place to rest. She had her priorities right – this was a man of God for whom she was caring. She had her husband's confidence and approval. She served Elisha willingly and without any thought of repayment or reciprocation. She provided shelter – nothing elaborate – a room with a bed, a table, a stool or chair, and a candlestick for light.

What hospitality actually to prepare a special room and furnish it for his use because she perceived him to be a man of God! No wonder the Bible describes her as a great woman.

Her example is still felt today. My husband and I have been guests in rooms that have been called by their owners the Elisha room or the prophet's room.

As the Greek word *"xenia"* implies, when you offer hospitality, you are giving a gift of lodging – shelter from the elements, shelter from the night, shelter from enemies.

SHELTER FROM THE ELEMENTS

In the chapter about the gift of nourishment, we noted how Paul had offered food and encouragement to his fellow shipmates after battling a storm and fasting for 14 days. Paul's hospitality was soon to be repaid by native islanders.

They found they had washed up on an island called Malta. In Acts 28:2, we read that the natives showed them extraordinary kindness. They kindled a fire and received all 276 of them and sheltered them from the rain and the cold. Even Publius, the chief man of the island, received them and lodged them for three days "courteously."

The next time you have drop-in company, remember the Malta islanders who had 276 soaking-wet, cold, hungry, dirty men, many of them convicts, show up unexpectedly and stay for three days.

SHELTER FROM THE NIGHT

Paul often relied on the hospitality of others for his shelter as he traveled. One such impromptu hostess was Lydia, a seller of purple in the city of Thyatira.

Paul and his traveling companions, after sailing from Troas to Samothrace and the next day to Neapolis, continued to Philippi in Macedonia where they stayed for several days. On the Sabbath day, they went outside the gate to a riverside to pray. Several women were assembled, and Paul began speaking to them.

One woman named Lydia, a seller of fine purple fabrics, was listening. Her heart was opened, and she responded to the teachings of Paul. After she and her household were baptized, she urged Paul and the other missionaries to share her home, saying, "If you have judged me to be faithful to the Lord, come into my house and stay," thus offering the gift of shelter to these traveling missionaries (Acts 16:15).

In this way, Lydia was a fellow worker with Paul. We have the same opportunities to help further the gospel by lodging mis-

sionaries when they come back to the states or visiting preachers
if they need a place to stay when conducting a meeting.

SHELTER FROM ENEMIES

Rahab gave hospitality to two spies sent by Joshua as protection
from their enemies, hiding them in her home although it put her
and her household in danger: "Then Joshua the son of Nun sent
two men as spies secretly from Shittim, saying, 'Go view the land,
especially Jericho.' So they went and came into the house of a harlot whose name was Rahab, and lodged there" (Joshua 2:1).

Rahab hid them in the stalks of flax that she had laid out on the
roof. And as a result, "Rahab the harlot and her father's household
and all she had, Joshua spared; and she has lived in the midst of
Israel to this day, for she hid the messengers whom Joshua sent
to spy out Jericho" (Joshua 6:25).

She gave her home for safety from the enemies of the spies. For
this she was mentioned among the heroes of faith in Hebrews 11:
"By faith Rahab the harlot did not perish along with those who were
disobedient, after she had welcomed the spies in peace" (v. 13).

FROM HOSTILITY TO HOSPITALITY

The jailer in Philippi paid little attention to his new charges.
These two men, Paul and Silas, were arrested for causing confu-
sion in the city by their teaching. They were not his concern; he
just put them into the inner prison as instructed and went to sleep.

The other prisoners took note of them, however. These two new
cellmates were not acting like the others sitting sullenly in their
cells. They were singing, of all things! Hadn't they just been beat-
en with rods? Hadn't their clothes been torn off by the angry mag-
istrates? But there they were in the inner prison, the one reserved
for the worst cases, with their feet fastened in those uncomfortable stocks – praying and singing!

As if this were not unusual enough, at midnight, the floor under
their feet began to shake. The earth rumbled, opening doors that
were meant to stay locked and releasing prisoners from their
chains. The jailer awakened in horror. He wasn't just afraid of losing his job; he was afraid of losing his life because there was no

way he could single-handedly recapture all the prisoners. Just as he was about to end it all, Paul called out to him, "Do yourself no harm, for we are all here" (Acts 16:28).

The jailer called for the lights and found, to his astonishment, that the other prisoners had remained in place, probably still curious about these two prayerful prisoners. He rushed into the inner prison and trembling fell down at the feet of Paul and Silas.

He was so relieved that within the hour, he carefully washed their wounds and began to listen to the teaching that had put them into his prison in the first place. He and his household were touched by their teaching and were baptized immediately. The hardened jailer became the hospitable host, taking them into his own home and setting food before them, rejoicing at the new turn his life had taken.

HOSPITALITY IN THE EARLY CHURCH

Paul writes, "Greet Prisca and Aquila, my fellow workers in Christ Jesus, who for my life risked their own necks, to whom not only do I give thanks, but also all the churches of the Gentiles; also greet the church that is in their house" (Romans 16:3-5). Another person who gave shelter to the church in his home was Gaius. Paul said, "Gaius, host to me and to the whole church, greets you" (v. 23).

Paul gives homage to an older man with whom he had stayed on his way to Jerusalem. "And some of the disciples from Caesarea also came with us, taking us to Mnason of Cyprus, a disciple of long standing ["an old disciple," KJV] with whom we were to lodge" (Acts 21:16). Although this disciple was perhaps advanced in age, he gave lodging to Paul and his companions.

HOSPITALITY TO CHILDREN

In our Wednesday night class recently, during the time for prayer requests, one of our university students asked for prayers for her sister's family. She explained that they, Scott and Amanda Smotherman of Savannah, Tenn., were adopting a sibling group of five children. As we collectively drew in our breath, she continued. The family already had four biological children of their own when they adopted an infant. In the year 2000 they heard about a Hispanic sibling group of six children that needed a home and adopted them.

Later they added an 18-year-old daughter and a 1-year-old son. So we were being asked to pray for them as they added this new sibling group of five, bringing the total to 18 children. Memphis-based AGAPE Child and Family Service reports that this may be the largest adoptive family in their 33 year history.

Families like this are a true inspiration to us. Although we may not have the same gift for this kind of service that the Smothermans do, we can all do something for children who need a family. Donations of money, labor and time are always appreciated by others who take in foster or adoptive children.

HOSPITALITY TO GOD

The only way we can show hospitality to God is to show it to others. God has no need of anything that we can give to Him. " 'Heaven is My throne, And earth is the footstool of My feet. What kind of house will you build for Me?' says the Lord; 'Or what place is there for My repose? Was it not My hand which made all these things?' " (Acts 7:49-50).

QUESTIONS

1. What are the Greek words that are translated as hospitality, and what does each mean?

2. In what ways did the Shunammite woman show her hospitality?

3. Why did Rahab merit mention among the heroes of faith in Hebrews 11?

4. Who offered shelter to the missionary after her baptism?

5. What man, perhaps even elderly, offered his home to Paul?

6. Who offered emergency shelter from the rain and cold?

SMALL GROUP DISCUSSIONS

1. Have you experienced the church meeting in a private home for worship service?

2. Like the island natives, have you experienced housing people in an emergency situation?

A KIND WORD

"Blessed are those who give without
remembering and take without forgetting."
Elizabeth Bibesco

"And if I give all my possessions to feed the poor, and
if I deliver my body to be burned, but do not have
love, it profits me nothing" (1 Corinthians 13:3).

"You have heard it said, 'An eye for an eye,
and a tooth for a tooth.' But I say to you,
do not resist him who is evil; but whoever
slaps you on your right cheek, turn to him
the other also. And if anyone wants to sue you,
and take your shirt, let him have your coat also.
And whoever shall force you to go one mile,
go with him two. Give to him who asks for you,
and do not turn away from him who wants
to borrow from you" (Matthew 5:38-42).

CHAPTER 7

"LET HIM HAVE YOUR CLOAK ALSO"

THE GIFT OF BENEVOLENCE, PART 1

"She stretches out her hands to the needy" (Proverbs 31:20).

Benevolence involves looking after the material needs of people. The Bible gives many examples of taking care of the needs of those less fortunate. The worthy woman described in Proverbs 31 is a great example of benevolence: "She extends her hand to the poor; And she stretches out her hands to the needy" (v. 20).

Paul wrote to the Romans that they should be "contributing to the needs of the saints, practicing hospitality" (Romans 12:13). Jesus taught us to make benevolence a priority. To the young man who asked how to have eternal life, Jesus explained, "One thing you lack: go and sell all you possess, and give to the poor, and you shall have treasure in heaven; and come, follow Me" (Mark 10:21).

Paul reminds us this also must be done with the right attitude: "And if I give all my possessions to feed the poor, and if I deliver my body to be burned, but do not have love, it profits me nothing" (1 Corinthians 13:3).

BENEVOLENT BOAZ

What a responsibility Ruth had taken on! The weight on her shoulders was as much emotional as physical. How could she, a new widow, possibly take care of her newly widowed mother-in-law who was grieving not only for her husband but also for the loss of her two sons. Yet Ruth was committed to care for Naomi, enough to leave her own country and follow Naomi to her people, her land. She would meet new people, establish a home, and attend to many other things. But her first concern was finding food.

Fortunately, it was spring, and the barley fields were ready for harvest. Moses' law taught that some of the produce of the fields was to be left for the poor and the strangers to glean; surely she would qualify on both counts. Ruth went in search of a field where she might find grain left by earlier gleaners.

By chance (or was it providence?), she came to the fields that belonged to Boaz, a wealthy relative of Naomi. She obtained permission from some of the servants to work there. When Boaz returned from Bethlehem, he noticed the new young woman and inquired about her. The servants explained she was a Moabite who had returned with Naomi.

Ruth must have wondered what Boaz was thinking when he called to her. Was she about to be scolded for trespassing? Her fears would soon be allayed. Boaz told her not to leave his fields but to follow his own maidens. When she was thirsty, she was to help herself to the water drawn by the young men who had been charged not to touch her.

This benevolent, protective spirit caused her to fall at Boaz's feet in gratitude, asking, "Why have I found favor in your sight that you should take notice of me, since I am a foreigner?" Boaz answered he had been told all that she had done for her mother-in-law in leaving her own country and kindred to come to a strange land. He said the Lord would surely bless her, and he further instructed her to come at mealtime and eat with the other reapers.

After Ruth left her meal to go back to work, Boaz commanded his young men to let her glean even among the sheaves without reproach. He said, "Let her glean even among the sheaves, and do not insult her. And also you shall purposely pull out for her some grain from the bundles and leave it that she may glean, and do not rebuke her" (Ruth 2:15-16). In this way, Boaz provided for the industrious Ruth without taking away her pride, privately making it easier for her to provide for herself and her dear mother-in-law.

The Bible says much about how we should treat the poor. The laws of the Old Testament protected the poor in various ways. In addition to Ruth's experience where owners of fields of grain were commanded to leave some for the poor to glean (Deuteronomy 24:19-22), other laws showed concern for the poor. The poor and needy servants were not to be oppressed but were to receive their wages before sundown, "for he is poor and sets his heart on it" (vv. 14-15). Every seventh year fields were to be left for the poor to harvest (Exodus 23:10-11).

GENEROUS JOB

When you think of Job, what attributes come to mind? Patience? Suffering? Certainly these apply. But another trait of Job was that of benevolence to the poor. In Job 31:16-22, we read:

> If I have kept the poor from their desire, Or have caused the eyes of the widow to fail, Or have eaten my morsel alone, And the orphan has not shared it
>
> (But from my youth he grew up with me as with a father, And from infancy I guided her),
>
> If I have seen anyone perish for lack of clothing, Or that the needy had no covering,
>
> If his loins have not thanked me, And if he has not been armed with the fleece of my sheep,
>
> If I have lifted up my hand against the orphan, Because I saw I had support in the gate,
>
> Let my shoulder fall from the socket, And my arm be broken off at the elbow.

TENDER-HEARTED TABITHA

One very benevolent woman was Tabitha, also known as Dorcas. In Acts 9:36, the Bible tells us that she was "full of good works and almsdeeds" (KJV). But Tabitha died and Peter went with some of the disciples to the place where Tabitha's body was lying. They took him into the upper room; there stood all the widows weeping and showing him the coats and garments that Tabitha made while she was alive. Here was a woman who looked after the material needs of others.

A very quiet and kindly man in our community passed away. He had been a handyman called on by so many of us when we had mechanical or plumbing problems. Lee Grantham believed his ministry was to take care of the widows and orphans. His fees were always modest, unless you were a widow; then he would not accept any payment at all.

He would repair a broken lamp, unclog a drain, or put new locks on a door. When the grateful lady would try to pay him, he refused, explaining, "The Bible says to visit the widows and the orphans, and this is my visit."

Lee gave us a visible example of "pure and undefiled religion" (James 1:27). At his funeral, we compared stories about Lee quietly doing acts of service for us, in the same way that the friends of Tabitha were showing the coats and garments she had made for them.

This attitude of benevolence is displayed in women today who host showers to help new mothers clothe their babies or new brides furnish their homes. We see people gather up sheets and blankets and clothing from their own homes to give victims of burnouts, tornadoes and floods. There are also the women who open their homes to care for foster children, meeting all their material needs as well as physical and emotional needs.

GIVING HOSPITALITY

Jesus reminds us that hospitality should not be shown only to those who can repay us but also to those who have no way of ever repaying:

> And He also went on to say to the one who had invited Him, "When you give a luncheon or a dinner, do not invite your friends or your brothers or your relatives or rich neighbors, lest they also invite you in return, and repayment come to you.
>
> But when you give a reception, invite the poor, the crippled, the lame, the blind, and you will be blessed,

since they do not have the means to repay you; for you will be repaid at the resurrection of the righteous" (Luke 14:12-14).

We should not expect to be paid back when we extend hospitality. My husband and I were impressed with a Christian couple we met in Bakersfield, Calif., Bob and Gloria Ford. After visiting in their home for a few minutes, they invited us to stay for dinner. We were reluctant, but they insisted.

At their table that evening were two others who were grateful for their hospitality. One was a blind man, and the other was a man whose wife was in the hospital for an extended stay. Neither of these men could repay the couple, but they were not expecting to be repaid. After dinner, the hostess took a plate of food to her next-door neighbor, a recent widow, who needed the companionship as much as the food.

WHAT LACK I YET?

The young man was earnest in his desire to be accepted by God. He had been listening to Jesus teach the crowds about the kingdom. As Jesus was about to leave, the young man must have felt something was missing in his own life, something that was holding him back from the blessed assurance of salvation. Seizing one last chance to hear from Jesus, he ran to Him and knelt before Him, asking:

"Good Teacher, what shall I do to inherit eternal life?" And Jesus said to him, "Why do you call Me good? No one is good except God alone. You know the commandments, 'Do not murder, Do not commit adultery, Do not steal, Do not bear false witness, Do not defraud, Honor your father and mother.' "

And he said to Him, "Teacher, I have kept all these things from my youth up." And looking at him, Jesus felt a love for him, and said to him, "One thing you lack: go and sell all you possess, and give to the poor, and you shall have treasure in heaven; and come, follow Me" (Mark 10:17-21).

Here at last the wealthy young man found the reason for his feeling of emptiness. He had laid up his treasure on earth, not sharing his wealth with others. Because he was not yet ready to change his life, he went away sorrowful.

FRUITS IN KEEPING WITH REPENTANCE

John came preparing the way for Christ, preaching to the people and urging them to repent of sins. He told them not to rely on the fact that they were the seed of Abraham but to "bring forth fruits in keeping with repentance" (Luke 3:8). When the people asked, "What should we do?" he told them, "Let the man who has two tunics share with him who has none; and let him who has food do likewise" (vv. 10-11). This attitude was to be one of the hallmarks of the Christian faith.

We find others in the New Testament who brought forth "fruits in keeping with repentance."

Cornelius, a centurion in Caesarea, was described as benevolent. He was "a devout man, and one who feared God with all his household, and gave many alms to the Jewish people, and prayed to God continually" (Acts 10:2).

Paul practiced the gift of benevolence. "I am going to Jerusalem serving the saints. For Macedonia and Achaia have been pleased to make a contribution for the poor among the saints in Jerusalem" (Romans 15:25-26).

The apostle John asked, "But whosoever has this world's goods, and beholds his brother in need and closes his heart against him, how does the love of God abide in him?" (1 John 3:17).

QUESTIONS

1. What does Paul teach us about the attitude we should have when giving to someone in need?

2. How did Boaz help Ruth without taking away her sense of pride?

3. What did the Mosaical law teach regarding one's grain fields?

4. In what other ways did the law protect the poor?

5. How did Job show hospitality to the poor?

6. What did John say was a "fruit in keeping with repentance"? What are some other fruits that he mentioned in that chapter?

7. What did the rich young ruler lack?

SMALL GROUP DISCUSSION

1. Who is a person in your community who exemplifies hospitality in looking after the needs of the unfortunate?

2. How can you find ways to help meet the material needs of others?

3. How can we "visit" the fatherless?

4. How can we "visit" the widows?

5. What should be our response to the poor?

A KIND WORD

"The heart benevolent and kind
The most resembles God."
Robert Burns

"Charity gives itself rich;
covetousness hoards itself poor."
German Proverb

"We lose what on ourselves we spend,
We have, as treasures without end,
Whatever, Lord, to thee we lend,
Who givest all – who givest all."
Christopher Wordsworth

"Justice begins with the recognition of
the necessity of sharing."
Elias Canetti

---------- CHAPTER 8 ----------

THE SIGNIFICANCE OF CLOTHING

—— THE GIFT OF BENEVOLENCE, PART 2 ——

"... naked, and you clothed Me."

In Chapter 7, we discussed how Tabitha made coats and garments for widows and orphans. From the time of Adam and Eve, clothing has served many purposes. The first and most obvious purpose is to cover our bodies. Often, when the Bible uses the term "naked," it means that the person was wearing only his inner garment or tunic.

We do like clothing, don't we? In the United States, clothing stores dominate every shopping mall. High fashion is big business. We marvel and often cringe at the attire worn by Hollywood's stars on the night of the Oscars. Even the worthy woman described in Proverbs made for herself "coverings of tapestry; her clothing is silk and purple" (31:22 KJV).

We women talk about clothes more than we would like to admit. Seeing a friend at church, we compliment her on her attire. "What a pretty dress you have on." "Oh, this? I've had this for two or three years!" "Well, it becomes you. You look good in red." It is the type of conversation repeated any time two women get together.

Each year, Freed-Hardeman University hosts a benefit dinner with a nationally known speaker. At one of these dinners, as my husband and I waited for the arrival of Elizabeth Dole, I wondered what we would talk about – maybe her work as president of the American Red Cross or her anticipated candidacy for president of the United States or even her husband's work as a U.S. senator. Finally, the anticipated moment arrived. She stepped out of the limousine dressed in a beautifully tailored business suit, smiling and confidently waving to the crowd. After going through the introductions to the university officials, she took me by the hand, leaned over and quietly whispered, "Am I dressed appropriately?" Suddenly we were just two women talking about clothes.

Jesus warns us not to be too preoccupied with clothing. As in so many things, balance is the key.

> For this reason I say to you, do not be anxious for your life, as to what you shall eat, or what you shall drink; nor for your body, as to what you shall put on. Is not life more than food, and the body more than clothing? ... And why are you anxious about clothing? Observe how the lilies of the field grow; they do not toil nor do they spin, yet I say to you that even Solomon in all his glory did not clothe himself like one of these (Matthew 6:25-29).

PREFERENTIAL TREATMENT CONDEMNED

James warns against holding an attitude of personal favoritism regarding people and their clothing.

> For if a man comes into your assembly with a gold ring and dressed in fine clothes, and there also comes in a poor man in dirty clothes, and you pay special attention to the one who is wearing the fine clothes, and say, "You sit here in a good place," and you say to the poor man, "You stand over there, or sit down by my footstool," have you not made distinctions among yourselves, and become judges with evil motives? (James 2:2-4).

Conversely, Jesus also warned us not to be like the Pharisees who used clothing to try to bring honor and respect to themselves. "Beware of the scribes who like to walk around in long robes, and like respectful greetings in the market places, and chief seats in the synagogues, and places of honor at banquets" (Mark 12:38-39).

Clothing in the United States is generally easy to acquire if the only purpose is to cover one's body. At any rummage sale or yard sale, some form of clothing can be obtained for pennies or even no cost at all. But a person's need for clothing goes beyond merely covering one's body. Protection from the elements, appropriate dress for the occasion, and boosting self-esteem are also reasons to provide clothing for those in need. It is interesting to look at the many references to clothing in the Bible.

PROTECTION FROM THE ELEMENTS

Clothing is important for protection against the weather. Without proper clothing, exposure to cold can cause injury or serious illness such as frostbite or hypothermia. The gracious people of the Granny White Church of Christ in Nashville, Tenn., are aware of the clothing needs in their own community. They conduct the "Warm Coats for Warm Hearts" drive each fall, collecting some 1,000 coats and jackets to be given away. These clean garments are sorted by size and neatly hung on racks. On the appointed November weekend people line up along the street leading to the church building waiting to shop for coats to fit themselves and their children. Other congregations across the country hold similar drives.

The law of Moses forbade keeping a person's coat from him at night when he needed protection from the elements. "If you ever take your neighbor's cloak as a pledge, you are to return it to him before the sun sets, for that is his only covering; it is his cloak for his body. What else shall he sleep in? And it shall come about that when he cries out to Me, I will hear him, for I am gracious" (Exodus 22:26-27).

APPROPRIATE DRESS

• In Jesus' parable of the wedding feast, we see that one's best attire was expected for formal occasions. "[W]hen the king came in to look over the dinner guests, he saw there a man not dressed in wedding clothes, and he said to him, 'Friend, how did you come in here without wedding clothes?' And he was speechless" (Matthew 22:11-12).

• When Pharaoh sent for Joseph to be brought to him from the dungeon, he did not come in the clothes he was wearing at the time, but "when he had shaved himself and changed his clothes, he came to Pharaoh" (Genesis 41:14).

• When Esther was persuaded to appear unbidden before the king to plead for her people, she dressed for the occasion. Esther knew that "for any man or woman who comes to the king to the inner court who is not summoned, he has but one law, that he be put to death, unless the king holds out to him the golden scepter so that he may live" (Esther 4:11). Esther's very life depended on her making a good impression.

> Now it came about on the third day that Esther put on her royal robes and stood in the inner court of the king's palace in front of the king's rooms, and the king was sitting on his royal throne in the throne room, opposite the entrance to the palace.
>
> And it happened when the king saw Esther the queen standing in the court, she obtained favor in his sight: and the king extended to Esther the golden scepter which was in his hand. So Esther came near, and touched the top of the scepter. Then the king said to her, "What is troubling you, Queen Esther? And what is your request? Even to half of the kingdom it will be given to you" (Esther 5:1-3).

TO BOOST SELF-ESTEEM

We must keep clothing in its proper perspective in our lives but also look out for the needs of others who may not have the type clothing they need. Clothing tells something about our self-esteem. A man or woman seeking employment needs to have clothing appropriate to the workplace. Children need clean and presentable clothing to help them feel they fit in with their peers. You may be able to make a difference in a person's life by supplying clothing suitable to the need.

CLOTHING USED AS A METAPHOR

• Isaiah speaks of "garments of vengeance for clothing" (59:17). He also speaks of the "garment of praise" (Isaiah 61:3 KJV) and writes, "I will rejoice greatly in the Lord, My soul will exult in my God; For He has clothed me with garments of salvation, He has wrapped me with a robe of righteousness, As a bridegroom decks himself with a garland, And as a bride adorns herself with her jewels" (v. 10).

• John compares acts of righteousness to beautiful clothing. "And it was given to her to clothe herself in fine linen, bright and clean; for the fine linen is the righteous acts of the saints" (Revelation 19:8).

• Job said, "I put on righteousness, and it clothed me; My justice was like a robe and a turban" (Job 29:14). Of the virtuous woman it is said, "Strength and dignity are her clothing; And she smiles at the future" (Proverbs 31:25).

MONETARY VALUE OF CLOTHING

Clothing was often given some monetary value. "And He said to them, 'But now, let him who has a purse take it along, likewise also a bag, and let him who has no sword sell his robe and buy one' " (Luke 22:36).

Jesus' seamless robe must have been considered of some value because the soldiers at the cross said, " 'Let us not tear it, but cast lots for it, to decide whose it shall be'; that the Scripture might be fulfilled, 'They divided my outer garments among them, and for My clothing they cast lots' " (John 19:24).

Clothing was also used as a gift, a reward or collateral.

• *A gift.* Abraham's servant went in search of a wife for Isaac, and upon finding Rebekah, he "brought out articles of silver and articles of gold, and garments, and gave them to Rebekah" (Genesis 24:53).

When Joseph was reunited with his brothers, he was overjoyed, and to "each of them he gave changes of garments, but to Benjamin he gave three hundred pieces of silver and five changes of garments" (Genesis 45:22).

After the last of 10 plagues was sent to the Egyptians, they were so glad to be rid of the Israelites that they allowed them to borrow clothing for their journey. "Now the sons of Israel had done according to the word of Moses, for they had requested from the Egyptians articles of silver and articles of gold, and clothing" (Exodus 12:35).

When Naaman went to Elisha the prophet to be healed of leprosy, he took with him gifts of "ten talents of silver and six thousand shekels of gold and ten changes of clothes" (2 Kings 5:5).

• *A reward.* When Joseph interpreted Pharaoh's dreams for him, "Pharaoh took off his signet ring from his hand, and put it on Joseph's hand, and clothed him in garments of fine linen, and put the gold necklace around his neck ... And he set him over all the land of Egypt" (Genesis 41:42-43).

Samson offered a reward to those who could solve his riddle. "Let me now propound a riddle to you; if you will indeed tell it to me within the seven days of the feast, and find it out, then I will give you thirty linen wraps and thirty changes of clothes" (Judges 14:12).

• *Collateral.* Clothing was even used as collateral. Moses instructed the Israelites, "If you ever take your neighbor's cloak as a pledge, you are to return it to him before the sun sets, for that is his only covering; it is his cloak for his body. What else shall he sleep in? And it shall come about that when he cries out to Me, I will hear him, for I am gracious" (Exodus 22:26-27).

DESIGNER GARMENTS

The priestly garments, which God designed for the priests and particularly the high priest, must have been works of art with their fringes and embroidered work on fine linen, in colors of white, blue, gold, purple and scarlet. Stones engraved with the names of the 12 tribes adorned the breastplate.

Beneath the hem hung pomegranates of blue, purple and scarlet alternating with bells of gold. These garments are described in Exodus 28:

> And you shall make holy garments for Aaron your brother, for glory and for beauty.
> And you shall speak to all the skillful persons whom I have endowed with the spirit of wisdom, that they

make Aaron's garments to consecrate him, that he may minister as priest to Me. And these are the garments which they shall make: a breastpiece and an ephod and a robe, and a tunic of checkered work, a turban and a sash, and they shall make holy garments for Aaron your brother and his sons, that he may minister as priests to Me (vv. 2-4).

When Aaron later rebelled against God, He told Moses to strip Aaron of this priestly garment.

Then the Lord spoke to Moses and Aaron at Mount Hor by the border of the land of Edom, saying, "Aaron shall be gathered to his people; for he shall not enter the land which I have given to the sons of Israel, because you rebelled against My command at the waters of Meribah. Take Aaron and his son Eleazar, and bring them up to Mount Hor; and strip Aaron of his garments and put them on his son Eleazar. So Aaron will be gathered to his people, and will die there" (Numbers 20:23-26).

COLOR CODED

Even the colors of garments are significant. Blue and purple are the colors that signify the wealth or royal standing of the wearer. According to *Unger's Bible Dictionary*, in biblical times, purple dye was extracted from a tiny shellfish, or mollusk, found along the Phoenician coast. The laborious extraction process made the dye so expensive that only royalty or the very wealthy could afford clothing of purple. Thus we read of the "purple robes which were on the kings of Midian" in Judges 8:26.

Blue is also sometimes referred to as a color for royalty. "Then Mordecai went out from the presence of the king in royal robes of blue and white" (Esther 8:15). Blue dye came from another species of shellfish and was also difficult to obtain.

Black clothing was used to indicate mourning. White garments often signified an angelic being. "But Mary was standing outside the tomb weeping; and so, as she wept, she stooped and looked into the tomb; and she beheld two angels in white sitting, one at the head, and one at the feet, where the body of Jesus had been lying" (John 20:11-12). Deity is also described as being clothed in white. When Jesus was transfigured, "His garments became radiant and exceedingly white, as no launderer on earth can whiten them" (Mark 9:3).

Saints in heaven will be clothed in white, perhaps signifying purity or holiness. "He who overcomes shall thus be clothed in white garments; and I will not erase his name from the book of life, and I will confess his name before My Father, and before His angels" (Revelation 3:5).

Even today, the color of our clothing denotes something of our mood and the occasion. Brides today still choose the traditional white to represent purity. Black is considered more formal or somber. Bright colors are worn to indicate a festive mood.

MISUSE OF CLOTHING

Soldiers used a kingly robe to make a mockery of Christ's deity. Pilate "took Jesus, and scourged Him. And the soldiers wove a crown of thorns and put it on His head, and arrayed Him in a purple robe; and they began to come up to Him, and say, 'Hail, King of the Jews!' and to give Him blows in the face" (John 19:1-3).

On one occasion, clothing was used to deceive. When the inhabitants of Gibeon heard that Joshua had defeated Jericho and Ai, they tricked Joshua into making a peace treaty with them by making him believe that they had traveled a long distance from their homes. They put on worn-out and patched sandals and worn-out clothing and carried with them dry crumbling bread, and said, "This our bread was warm when we took it for our provisions out of our houses on the day that we left to come to you" (Joshua 9:12). Their deception worked. Joshua made a covenant with these people who were already living in the land of the Israelites.

Another misuse of clothing occurs when men and women intentionally try to deceive people concerning their gender identity. "A woman shall not wear man's clothing, nor shall a man put on a woman's clothing; for whoever does these things is an abomination to the Lord your God" (Deuteronomy 22:5).

Paul put clothing into perspective for us when he wrote to Timothy,

"Likewise, I want women to adorn themselves with proper clothing, modestly and discreetly, not with braided hair and gold or pearls or costly garments; but rather by means of good works, as befits women making a claim to godliness" (1 Timothy 2:9-10).

COAT OF MANY QUARRELS

Seventeen-year-old Joseph was the apple of his father's eye. Jacob was in his later years when Joseph was born, and his father doted on him. He gave Joseph a beautiful tunic or coat of many colors. This coat must have taken much effort to make as each change of color represented time spent in dyeing the separate colors and weaving them into fabric.

The brothers certainly took notice of this coat and began to hate Joseph so much they couldn't even speak to him in a friendly way. It wasn't just the coat that made them angry; it represented the favoritism that their father expressed through the gift of this beautiful piece of clothing (Genesis 37:3-4).

MIRACULOUS WARDROBE

After fleeing Egypt, the Israelites wandered 40 years in the wilderness. Moses reminded them that during those 40 years their clothing and sandals did not wear out (Deuteronomy 29:5-6).

Jesus' garments were made special because of the person wearing them. "And wherever He entered villages, or cities, or countryside, they were laying the sick in the marketplaces, and entreating Him that they might just touch the fringe of His cloak; and as many as touched it were being cured" (Mark 6:56).

CLOTHING TO SIGNIFY EMOTION

• *Sorrow and Penitence.* Clothing made of sackcloth was used to denote sorrow or penitence. Sackcloth was a coarse, textured cloth made of goat's hair. The person's physical discomfort matched his or her emotional discomfort.

John the Baptist wore a garment made of camel's hair (Matthew 3:4), perhaps to call attention to his message of repentance and mourning over sins.

In the story of Esther, the king issued a decree "to destroy, to kill, and to annihilate all the Jews, both young and old, women and children, in one day" (Esther 3:13). Kill, destroy and annihilate – three ways of expressing the same horrid idea. Mordecai, upon learning of this decree, "tore his clothes, put on sackcloth and ashes, and went out into the midst of the city and wailed loudly and bitterly" – three expressions of his grief and anguish (4:1).

The king of Nineveh, after hearing the words of Jonah, proclaimed: "But both man and beast must be covered with sackcloth; and let men call on God earnestly that each may turn from his wicked way and from the violence which is in his hands" (Jonah 3:8).

King Josiah tore his garments after hearing the book of the law read "because our fathers have not listened to the words of this book, to do according to all that is written concerning us" (2 Kings 22:13).

David wrote, "Thou hast turned for me my mourning into dancing; Thou hast loosed my sackcloth and girded me with gladness" (Psalm 30:11).

Jesus said, "Woe to you, Chorazin! Woe to you, Bethsaida! For if the miracles had occurred in Tyre and Sidon which occurred in you, they would have repented long ago in sackcloth and ashes" (Matthew 11:21).

• *Grief.* Certain garments were used to denote widowhood. Tamar "removed her veil and put on her widow's garments" (Genesis 38:19). In recent history, the wearing of the color black is used to signify mourning – a somber color for a somber feeling.

• *Happiness.* Clothing is sometimes used to show happier emotions. When the prodigal son returned home, his father said to his servants: " 'Quickly bring out the best robe and put it on him, and put a ring on his hand and sandals on his feet; and bring the fattened calf, kill it, and let us eat and be merry; for this son of mine was dead, and has come to life again; he was lost, and has been found.' And they began to be merry" (Luke 15:22-24).

• *Praise.* According to *Unger's Bible Dictionary*, "The spreading of garments in the streets before persons to whom it was intended to show particular honor was a very ancient and general custom." When Jesus made His triumphant entry into Jerusalem riding on a donkey, He sat on an improvised saddle of sorts. The disciples had

> brought the donkey and the colt, and laid on them their garments, on which He sat. And most of the multitude spread their garments in the road, and others were cutting branches from the trees, and spreading them in the road. And the multitudes going before Him, and those who followed after were crying out, saying, "Hosanna to the Son of David; Blessed is He who comes in the name of the Lord; Hosanna in the highest!" (Matthew 21:7-9).

Similarly, when Jehu was made king "each man took his garment and placed it under him on the bare steps, and blew the trumpet, saying, 'Jehu is king!'" (2 Kings 9:13).

• *Sentimentality.* Even today, clothing can have a special significance. What bride can forget the dress she wore on her wedding day? I treasure a hand-crocheted baby dress made by my grandmother and carefully kept by my mother. The dress has now been worn by me, my daughter and my granddaughter, threading its way through five generations.

Clothing has long been considered a thing of value and significance. It says something about who we are, about how we feel. It warms our bodies. It affects our self-esteem. Although we are not to be preoccupied with our own clothing nor give preferential treatment based on another's attire, it is still important for people to have appropriate clothing. Jesus said, "I was naked, and you clothed Me." The only way we can do this is to look after the clothing needs of others.

QUESTIONS

1. Aside from the obvious need for covering one's nakedness, what other functions does clothing serve?

2. What are some warnings we are given regarding the importance we place on clothing?

3. How has clothing been used to reflect one's emotions?

4. How does the Bible describe the priestly garments in the Old Testament?

5. How was Jesus mocked with an article of clothing?

SMALL GROUP DISCUSSION

1. What are some ways you can help provide clothing to those who need it?

2. Do you have a garment that has great sentimental value to you? Why is it important?

A KIND WORD

"Blessed be the God and Father of our
Lord Jesus Christ, the Father of mercies
and God of all comfort" (2 Corinthians 1:3).

"He stands erect by bending over the fallen.
He rises by lifting others."
Robert Green Ingersoll

"God gave burdens, also shoulders."
Yiddish Proverb

"It is a kingly act to assist the fallen."
Ovid

"Bear one another's burdens" (Galatians 6:2).

CHAPTER 9

BEAR ONE ANOTHER'S BURDENS

THE GIFT OF COMFORT

"I was sick, and you visited Me."

The word "visit" in Matthew 25:36 means so much more than the way we commonly use it today. We often refer to a social call as a visit. But the Greek word for visit, *"episkeptomai,"* carries with it the idea of looking after others, attending to their need for comfort. This is the word used in James 1:27: "This is pure and undefiled religion in the sight of our God and Father, to visit orphans and widows in their distress, and to keep oneself unstained by the world." The same word is used when Jesus said, "I was sick, and you visited Me" (Matthew 25:36).

Caring for the sick was highly esteemed among the Jews. Adam Clarke's commentary relates one of their sayings on this subject: " 'He who neglects to visit the sick is like him who has shed blood.' That is, as he has neglected, when it was in his power, to preserve life, he is as guilty in the sight of the Lord as he is who has committed murder" (822).

The English word "hospitality" has a long history of connection with the practice of caring for the sick. We get our English word "hospital" from the same medieval Latin word for guest or guest room.

COMFORT FOR THE CHRONICALLY ILL, THE HANDICAPPED AND THE AGED

There is perhaps no greater service than caring for someone who is chronically ill, handicapped or aged. This is truly a sacrifice of time, energy and resources. According to the Office on Women's Health in the Department of Health and Human Services:

• About one-fourth of American families are caring for an older family member, an adult child with disabilities, or a friend.

• According to recent surveys, more than 7 million persons are informal caregivers to older adults. Caregivers include spouses, adult children, and other relatives and friends. Other surveys found that almost 26 million family caregivers provide care to adults (aged 18-plus) with a disability or chronic illness, and 5 million informal caregivers provide care for older adults aged 50-plus with dementia.

• Studies show that more than half of caregivers are women. Care receivers are about half women and half men.

• The average amount of time that caregivers spend on caregiving is about 20 hours per week. Even more time is required when the care receiver has multiple disabilities.

"Caregiver Stress" is the name given to the list of symptoms common among those who have round-the-clock responsibilities such as assisting another person with dressing, feeding, bathing, transportation and grocery shopping. Symptoms include depression, guilt, headaches, frustration and anger. Caregivers are also more likely to become physically ill.

• As a caregiver, you can take steps to take care of your own health: Eat a healthy diet rich in fruits, vegetables and whole grains and low in saturated fat. Ask your health care provider about taking a multivitamin as well.

• Try to get enough sleep and rest. Find time for some exercise most days of the week. Regular exercise can help reduce stress and improve your health in many ways. See your health care provider for a checkup. Talk to your provider about symptoms of depression or illness that you may be having. Get counseling if needed.

• Stay in touch with friends. Social activities can help keep you feeling connected and help with stress. Faith-based groups can offer support and help to caregivers.

• Find a support group for other caregivers in your situation (such as caring for a person with dementia). Many support groups are available online through the Internet.

If you are the person receiving the care, any words of appreciation and thankfulness will help relieve stress and make the caregiver's job more pleasant. As Christians we should remember to give attention not only to the sick and afflicted, but also to the caregiver.

In our mobile society, we often live far away from our own relatives. Friends become much more precious to us when we have no family close by in time of sickness. "Better is a neighbor who is near than a brother far away" (Proverbs 27:10). We must comply with the biblical injunction to "[b]ear one another's burdens" (Galatians 6:2).

In 2 Samuel, we read of David's desire to repay a kindness to Jonathan. He asked:

> "Is there not yet anyone of the house of Saul to whom I may show the kindness of God?" And Ziba said to the king, "There is still a son of Jonathan who is crippled in both feet." So the king said to him, "Where is he?" And Ziba said to the king, "Behold, he is in the house of Machir the son of Ammiel in Lo-debar." Then King David sent and brought him from the house of Machir the son of Ammiel, from Lo-debar. And Mephibosheth, the son of Jonathan the son of Saul, came to David and fell on his face and prostrated himself. And David said, "Mephibosheth." And he said, "Here is your servant!" And David said to him, "Do not fear, for I will surely show kindness to you for the sake of your father Jonathan, and will restore to you all the land of your grandfather Saul; and you shall eat at my table regularly" (2 Samuel 9:3-7).

Great strides have been made in making our nation more hospitable to the handicapped. Doubtless, more needs to be done. Handicaps come in all varieties and ranges. If you have an acquaintance who is handicapped, remember to treat him or her with the same respect you would treat anyone else. Ask what can be done to make them more comfortable in your home, and be happy to assist if they need assistance.

COMFORT FOR THE WOUNDED

Jesus spent much of His time healing the sick because He felt compassion. He used a parable about compassion for the wounded to explain the concept of loving our neighbor. In Luke 10:25, a certain lawyer tried to test Jesus by asking, "Teacher, what shall I do to inherit eternal life?" Jesus answered, "What is written in the law? How does it read to you?"

The lawyer knew the law and answered, "You shall love the Lord your God with all your heart, and with all your soul, and with all your strength, and with all your mind; and your neighbor as yourself." Jesus said, "You have answered correctly; do this and you will live."

The lawyer wanted to justify himself, so he asked, "And who is my neighbor?" Jesus answered by telling this story:

> A certain man was going down from Jerusalem to Jericho; and he fell among robbers, and they stripped him and beat him, and went off leaving him half dead.
>
> And by chance a certain priest was going down on that road, and when he saw him, he passed by on the other side. And likewise a Levite also, when he came to the place and saw him, passed by on the other side.
>
> But a certain Samaritan, who was on a journey, came upon him; and when he saw him, he felt compassion, and came to him, and bandaged up his wounds, pouring oil and wine on them; and he put him on his own beast, and brought him to an inn, and took care of him. And on the next day he took out two denarii and gave them to the innkeeper and said, "Take care of him; and

whatever more you spend, when I return, I will repay
you " (Luke 10:30-35).

Then Jesus answered the lawyer's question with a question of
His own. "Which of these three do you think proved to be a neighbor to the man who fell into the robbers' hands?"

The lawyer answered, "The one who showed mercy toward him."
And Jesus simply said, "Go and do the same" (Luke 10:36-37).

It has been said that the reactions of the robber, the priest and
Levite and the Samaritan represent three philosophies of life. The
robber's philosophy was, "What's thine is mine." The priest and
Levite believed, "What's thine is thine and what's mine is mine."
But the Samaritan's philosophy was, "What's mine is thine."

COMFORT FOR VICTIMS OF CIRCUMSTANCE

In May 2003, a tornado ripped through Jackson, Tenn., a town
just a few miles north of our hometown. Hundreds of homes were
destroyed. Church buildings, schools and the U.S. Post Office appeared as though they had been bombed.

Almost immediately, 24 emergency shelters were set up in school
gymnasiums and other appropriate structures. Volunteers from
neighboring counties served meals, provided clothing, bedding
and emotional support to thousands of victims.

Disasters like this call for immediate and organized assistance.
Christians have the opportunity to show the love of Christ to those
who are suffering. There is something that almost anyone can do
– collect and distribute clothing, donate funds, serve meals, help
clean up debris, or offer transportation to those whose vehicles
have been damaged. The simplest act of kindness can reassure
victims that they are not alone and that they can survive.

In chapter 3, we left Paul a prisoner on a storm-tossed sailing
vessel breaking bread with his guards and fellow travelers. After
they had eaten, they began to lighten the ship further by throwing the rest of their wheat overboard.

The next morning, although they did not recognize the land,
they could see a bay with a beach. They decided to take desper-
ate measures and drive the ship onto it if possible. Unfortunately,
they struck a reef and wrecked the ship.

The soldiers planned to kill the prisoners so they would not be held responsible for their escape. But the centurion who wanted to bring Paul safely through gave orders for everyone to jump overboard and swim or ride on planks or other material from the ship to get to land. The plan was successful, and, just as the angel of God had foretold, not one of them was lost.

These victims of the violent storm and shipwreck found themselves on the island of Malta. Although Paul was not sick, as our chapter suggests, he certainly was in need of care and comfort. Tired from the strenuous swim to shore, he was cold from the rains that had followed the storm. To their great credit, the natives were hospitable to Paul and the other prisoners and showed extraordinary kindness, building a fire to warm them. Paul pitched in to help, and as he picked up a bundle of sticks and laid them on the fire, a viper came out and bit his hand.

Just when he must have thought nothing more could happen to him, the people added insult to injury by suggesting that Paul must be a murderer for this viper to bite him therefore serving justice on him. After waiting a long time and seeing that he did not fall dead from the snakebite, they changed their minds to the opposite extreme, deciding that he must be a god.

Finally, Paul's misfortunes were behind him. The chief man of the islands, Publius, showed great hospitality when he welcomed and entertained Paul courteously for three days. When Publius' father became ill, Paul was able to repay the kindnesses shown to him by praying, laying on hands, and healing this man (Acts 27:1-28:10). As often is the case, we cannot repay the people who have helped us, but we can pass along the kindness to others.

Paul and his co-workers were often in need of comfort. At one point he said: we are afflicted in every way ... we are perplexed ... we are persecuted ... we are struck down ... .

But this is only half of what he said. He also stated: ... but not crushed ... but not despairing ... but not forsaken ... but not destroyed (2 Corinthians 4:7-9).

The reason he could add the second half of the phrases was because of the "One who has shone in our hearts" (2 Corinthians 4:6).

GOD'S EXAMPLE OF COMFORT

Paul wrote about the God of all comfort "who comforts us in all our affliction so that we may be able to comfort those who are in any affliction with the comfort with which we ourselves are comforted by God" (2 Corinthians 1:4).

Anyone who has endured an illness or a crisis knows how much a small act can mean. A container of homemade stew brought to your door can comfort in ways that the finest meal in a five-star restaurant cannot do. A quick hug around the shoulders can reassure you that someone remembers your troubles. A short but meaningful note can be read and reread when you need it most.

Jesus said, "The Spirit of the Lord is upon Me, Because He anointed Me to preach the gospel to the poor. He has sent Me to proclaim release to the captives, And recovery of sight to the blind, To set free those who are downtrodden, To proclaim the favorable year of the Lord" (Luke 4:18). He came to offer hospitality to the needy, the imprisoned, the hurting and the downtrodden. It is up to us to make sure that mission is carried out.

Jesus taught Simon Peter the importance of taking care of others. After Jesus' disciples had enjoyed the breakfast of fish and bread that Jesus had prepared for them, Jesus looked at Peter and asked him, "Simon … do you love Me?" Peter replied that he did. Jesus said, "Tend My lambs" (John 21:15). Jesus repeated the question twice more, with the same admonition to feed or tend His sheep.

Jesus is reminding Peter that one's love for Him is connected to our responsibility to love and tend to those who belong to Him. Jesus not only prepared their breakfast for them, He also had told the fishermen just where to cast their nets to have their nets overflowing with fish. He gives abundantly to us and reminds us that we can show our love and appreciation by tending to the needs of others.

QUESTIONS

1. What does it mean to visit in the fullest sense?

2. Can you identify seven acts of hospitality the Samaritan performed for the injured man?

3. How much would two denari be worth?

4. What misfortunes did Paul experience, causing him to need care and comfort?

5. How did the islanders care for Paul?

6. How did Paul keep a positive attitude in the middle of so many trials and troubles?

7. What did the Spirit of the Lord anoint Jesus to do?

SMALL GROUP DISCUSSION
1. Can you think of a kindness that has been done to you that you can repay only by passing it on to others?

2. Do you have special needs? What can others do to lighten your load?

3. Can you think of a time when even a small act of kindness made a big difference in your life?

4. Although we are told to bear one another's burdens, we are also told to bear our own (Galatians 6:5). One way we can do this is to give direction to our families in the event that we become unable to help ourselves. What ways can help our families in such a difficult time? How might having a will make be a blessing to our families?

A KIND WORD

"Better is a neighbor who is near than a
brother who is far away" (Proverbs 27:10b).

"Not what we give, but what we share,
for the gift without the giver is bare."
J.R. Lowell

"While there is a lower class, I am in it.
While there is a criminal class I am of it.
While there is a soul in prison I am not free."
A. Powell Davies, Ethical Outlook

"Oh, a friend! How true is that old saying,
that the enjoyment of one is sweeter and more necessary
than that of the elements of water and fire!"
Michel de Montaigne

"No act of kindness, no matter how small,
is ever wasted."
Aesop

CHAPTER 10

GIVING OF YOURSELF

THE GIFT OF COMPANIONSHIP

"I was in prison, and you came to Me."

Helen Keller, who had limited sensory contact with others because of her blindness and deafness, wrote about human touch, "I have met people so empty of joy, that when I clasped their frosty finger-tips, it seemed as if I were shaking hands with a northeast storm. Others there are whose hands have sunbeams in them, so that their grasp warms my heart. It may be only the clinging touch of a child's hand, but there is as much potential sunshine in it for me as there is in a longing glance for others."

Our Lord promised us companionship. "Let your conversation be without covetousness; and be content with such things as ye have: for he hath said, I will never leave thee, nor forsake thee" (Hebrews 13:5 KJV). He also promised "I am with you always, even to the end of the age" (Matthew 28:20 NASB).

We receive this gift of companionship when someone invites us over for a meal or a cup of coffee and spends time conversing and getting to know us better. Ralph Waldo Emerson said, "The greatest gift is a portion of thyself."

"I WAS IN PRISON"

All of us long for companionship. Human beings were made to be in contact with other human beings. In the prisons of most civilized countries, physical needs are taken care of even when one is ill. One who is imprisoned is presumably fed, clothed and sheltered. But what may be lacking is companionship with people in the world outside and non-judgmental acceptance.

The gift of companionship was given to Paul when he was in prison: "The Lord grant mercy to the house of Onesiphorus for he often refreshed me, and was not ashamed of my chains; but when he was in Rome, he eagerly searched for me, and found me – the Lord grant to him to find mercy from the Lord on that day – and you know very well what services he rendered at Ephesus" (2 Timothy 1:16-18). Paul was grateful for Onesiphorus because he often refreshed him and was not ashamed of his imprisonment.

Here are three suggestions for us in helping prisoners.

• First, refresh them with visits, not just once, but often. Writing letters to those who are in prison is another way of offering companionship. They are hungry for the companionship and guidance of people outside their walls.

• Second, help them preserve their dignity. It is significant that Paul mentions Onesiphorus was "not ashamed" of his chains. This does not mean acceptance of the wrong, but of the person. If someone you know is in prison, you may also be able to help attend to the needs of the family left behind. Often these innocent victims of their loved one's imprisonment are shunned and made to feel ashamed of their circumstances.

• Third, we can also pray for the release of prisoners who have been imprisoned for religious persecution or falsely accused of wrongdoing. When Peter was in prison, a group of friends met at the home of John Mark's mother to pray. Miraculously, their prayer was answered as an angel appeared to Peter telling him to follow. The chains fell off his arms; he dressed himself and followed, not knowing whether he was seeing a vision or reality. Only after he walked outside the prison gates between two sleeping guards did he begin to realize it was really happening.

He went to the house where his friends were praying for him. Rhoda, the servant-girl, answered his knock at the gate and was so joyful she ran back to the house without opening the gate, leaving Peter literally standing out in the night. She ran in and interrupted their prayers with the news that Peter was at the gate. Not believing their prayers could have been answered so quickly, they said, "You are out of your mind!" But when they opened the door, they saw him still knocking at the gate and they were amazed (Acts 12:1-16).

PRISONS WITHOUT WALLS

We often think of a prison as a gray, concrete building surrounded by high fences and barbed wire. But some prisons have no walls.

David prayed for deliverance from his prison of fear. "I cried out to Thee, O Lord; I said, 'Thou are my refuge, My portion in the land of the living. Give heed to my cry, For I am brought very low; Deliver me from my persecutors, For they are too strong for me. Bring my soul out of prison, So that I may give thanks to Thy name'" (Psalm 142:5-7).

Some people are locked up in grief over the death of a loved one. Taking food to the family is a way of giving hospitality. We should remember to mention the name of the deceased to his or her loved ones rather than act as though that person had never existed. On the first Father's Day after my dad passed away, friends made a call or sent a card to say that they were thinking of me. What a sweet and thoughtful gesture that was.

Others need someone who will take the time to listen to and give counsel to those who need emotional support. Hubert Humphrey observed, "The greatest healing therapy is friendship and love."

A PRISONER OF LONELINESS

Many people are in prisons of loneliness, people who would love companionship even if just for an evening. It might be a widow or widower. Some are lonely because of distance from loved ones – a homesick college student or exchange students from foreign countries. To be invited into someone's home is an honor, and we are commanded to show honor to one another. Young men and women in service stationed away from home and missionaries need our companionship, too, through letters, a box of candy or some other remembrance.

Sometimes, the gift of companionship is as simple as speaking to another person, by acknowledging the existence of another. Ryan LaHurd, former president of Lenoir-Rhyne College in North Carolina, wrote about an experience he had as young man entering the University of Chicago. The route he walked from his residence to his classes took him through a rough neighborhood. He was a bit anxious as he passed run-down buildings and trash-strewn streets.

Passing by an old apartment building, he saw a man sitting on the steps. The unshaven man was dressed in stained and torn clothing. "Good morning, son," the man called out.

I didn't know what to do, so I just kept walking, saying nothing, LaHurd wrote. Just as I was leaving, I heard the old man say, "I'm Daleestadees!"

LaHurd thought that was an odd Greek-sounding name and felt a little guilty about ignoring him, especially because he was offering his name in greeting. But you just can't be too careful, he decided.

All day the memory of Daleestades invaded his thoughts. The next morning he had to pass the same way. As luck would have it, the old man was sitting in the same doorway. Trying not to notice him, he crossed the street to avoid meeting Daleestades again. But the old man motioned to him, and he felt it would be terribly impolite to ignore him, so he crossed back.

The man spoke, "I said, 'Good morning, son,'" repeating the greeting he had made the day before.

Reluctantly LaHurd answered, "Good morning, Daleestades." The old man started to laugh and said, "No, my name is Albert. Yesterday when you ignored my friendly greeting, I used part of a Bible verse: 'What you do to da leasta deez my brethren, you do to me.' I just wanted to say, I'm your brother."

Taking the time to really get to know people helps us to understand and love them more.

THE LONELIEST BOY IN SCHOOL

"Mom, today I met the loneliest boy in school," was the announcement made by Ed to his mother as he came through the doors of his home in Michigan. The boy to whom he referred was George, a new student in Ed's class.

George had reason to be lonely. George's mother died when he was 5 years old. He and his nine siblings were farmed out to different homes. The oldest brother and sister, at ages 16 and 17, struck out on their own to find jobs. Six others were placed in two different orphan homes. George and his youngest sister were sent to live with an aunt and later were sent back home to live with his father and new stepmother.

Although George was happy to be back home, his life was far from peaceful. His father, a railroad engineer, was an alcoholic. When his father became ill with cancer, George went to live with a sister in Michigan. He found the regional differences to be paramount to living in a foreign country and was grateful to find another displaced Southerner in his new friend Ed.

Ed's mother encouraged him to make friends with this lonely boy, and the family asked him to attend church with them. George was baptized as a senior in high school, giving him a spiritual family.

Later, Ed's mother encouraged George to think about college. He really didn't know how he would manage it. Through her persistence, George obtained scholarships that enabled him to go to college where he met and married his bride and obtained his degree.

What a difference this gift of companionship made in George's life. He is now passing on this act of kindness by endowing a scholarship for others who want to go to college.

LONELY IN A CROWD

Sometimes we find ourselves in a position of loneliness because we don't believe we fit in. In a world of couples, the single or widowed may feel awkward in groups, particularly in churches where families tend to sit together. How can we help them feel a companionship with us?

A friend who is single again gives these suggestions:
- Talk to them! Don't let fear of offending keep you from showing your love and concern.
- Call and visit, especially after the crisis times are over, but the pain isn't.
- Be available to listen, listen, listen.
- Use the sense of touch – a touch on the shoulder or a hug works wonders.
- Take them out to lunch.
- Send cards of encouragement.
- Sit with them at church services.
- Go with them when asked.
- Remember special days: birthdays, anniversaries of loss, etc.
- Include them in activities with couples. Even if they do not want to come, they appreciate being asked.

FINDING COMPANIONSHIP

One way for a lonely person to find companionship is to seek others who need it also. Letha Burleson, a lovely widow, had this poem on her refrigerator door:

> Seldom can a heart be lonely
> If it seeks a lonelier still,
> Self-forgetting, seeking only
> Emptier cups to fill.

Letha follows the advice in the poem. She is constantly helping others. She spends time every summer on a campaign on Christmas Island in the Pacific teaching Bible classes to the native women. She often brings several freshly baked apple pies in the trunk of her car to give away when she visits.

She certainly meets Paul's description of the hospitable widow. He says we should care for a widow if she is: "Well reported of for good works [*the gift of benevolence*]; if she have brought up children, if she have lodged strangers [*the gift of shelter*], if she have washed the saints' feet [*the gift of service*], if she have relieved the afflicted [*the gift of comfort*], if she have diligently followed every good work" [*the gift of benevolence*] (1 Timothy 5:10 KJV).

COMPANIONSHIP AT HOME

We also have a responsibility to provide companionship for our own families, not neglecting them to serve others. A sad commentary is seen in this statement: "[T]hey made me the keeper of the vineyards; but mine own vineyard have I not kept" (Song of Solomon 1:6 KJV).

Timothy's mother and grandmother gave companionship to young Timothy, and it had a profound effect on him. Timothy was the kind of person he was, full of unfeigned faith, because his mother and grandmother spent time with him.

Paul wrote to Timothy: "For I am mindful of the sincere faith within you, which first dwelt in your grandmother Lois, and your mother Eunice, and I am sure that it is in you as well" (2 Timothy 1:5 NASB).

Seated next to a minister at dinner one evening, I asked him who influenced him to become a minister. He smiled and said, "As early as I can remember, even as my mother was dressing me, she would say, 'Your uncle is a very important man. He is a doctor. But your father is even more important. He is a preacher.' And from that time on I knew that I wanted to be a minister like my dad."

COMPANIONS OF JESUS

Mary, Martha and Lazarus offered this gift of companionship to Jesus. He apparently enjoyed staying in their home. "Now Jesus loved Martha, and her sister, and Lazarus" (John 11:5).

Jesus contrasted the hospitality of Martha and Mary: "But the Lord answered and said to her, 'Martha, Martha, you are worried and bothered about so many things; but only a few things are necessary, really only one, for Mary has chosen the good part, which shall not be taken away from her' " (Luke 10:41).

Mary, in particular, showed her interest in Jesus by listening intently to His teaching. It was Mary who had shown her hospitality by anointing Jesus with ointment and wiping His feet with her hair (John 11:2).

As we share hospitality with other Christians, We "kindle afresh the gift of God" (2 Timothy 1:6) as if we were stirring up the embers of a fire. We encourage one another unto good works.

Hospitality is giving the gift of companionship and human contact and meeting the spiritual and emotional needs of others.

QUESTIONS

1. How did Onesiphorus act hospitably toward Paul? What three things can we learn from him regarding prisoners?

2. How can grandparents be good companions to their grand-children?

3. Contrast the hospitality and companionship of Mary and Martha to Jesus.

4. How can we help someone serving a prison sentence?

5. How did Jesus promise us companionship?

SMALL GROUP DISCUSSION

1. Is there a prison ministry in your area?

2. What can be done for the families of someone who is in prison?

3. What groups of people can you think of who need the gift of companionship?

A KIND WORD

"[F]or I was hungry, and you gave Me nothing to eat; I was thirsty, and you gave Me nothing to drink: I was a stranger, and you did not invite Me in; naked, and you did not clothe Me; sick, and in prison, and you did not visit Me" (Matthew 25:42-43).

"Four things come not back: the spoken word; the sped arrow; time past; the neglected opportunity."
Omer ibn al-Halif

"Opportunities are like sunrises.
If you wait too long, you miss them."
William Arthur Ward

CHAPTER 11

MISSED OPPORTUNITIES

"Truly I say to you, to the extent that you
did not do it to one of the least of these,
you did not do it to Me" (Matthew 25:45).

In the days of Caesar Augustus, a census was decreed for the inhabitants of the Roman empire. All the citizens were required to go to their own city to register. This posed a problem for young Mary and Joseph because traveling was difficult in her final stage of pregnancy. After making the journey, they discovered there was no room for them in the inn.

We really don't know if Joseph and Mary talked to the innkeeper, and it would be easy for us to assume that the innkeeper was a heartless individual to turn away this young couple. But remember, he was probably overrun with requests for rooms because of the unusually large crowds of people coming into town for the purpose of registering. Most likely, he had already turned away several.

Had the innkeeper only known that the baby to be born and placed in a manger that night was to be the King of kings, he most certainly would have given up his own bed for such a guest. It was a missed opportunity to extend hospitality.

DENYING HOSPITALITY TO JESUS

A Pharisee named Simon invited Jesus into his home for a meal. Seemingly, he was being quite hospitable. But things are not always as they appear. Simon did not follow the accepted rules of etiquette toward his guest. He did not offer Jesus water with which to wash His feet, dusty from travel. He did not offer Him the customary kiss of greeting. He did not even anoint Him with oil, a practice as common among the Jews as it would be for us to offer a guest the opportunity to freshen up before a meal.

David, in one of his psalms said, "Thou preparest a table before me … thou anointest my head with oil" (Psalm 23:5 KJV). Whether these omissions were an oversight or a deliberate slight by Simon, they were inexcusable to such an honored guest.

However, one woman in Simon's home had an entirely different reaction to the presence of Jesus from that of the Pharisee. She stood behind Him as He reclined at the table and washed His feet with her tears and wiped them with her long, flowing hair. She kissed His feet, which was a practice among the heathen people, indicating subjection and adoration. She then took her own alabaster box of ointment and began to anoint His feet.

Taking note of this, Simon muttered to himself, "If this man were a prophet He would know who and what sort of person this woman is and who is touching Him, that she is a sinner."

Jesus, perceiving Simon's reaction, said, "Simon, I have something to say to you." Simon listened as Jesus told a parable of two debtors. One owed 50 denari, and the other owed 10 times that amount. Their creditor, seeing that they were unable to repay him, forgave their debt. Jesus then asked, "Which of them therefore will love him more?" Simon answered and said, "I suppose the one whom he forgave more."

Jesus told Simon he had answered correctly. He went on to teach Simon (and us) a valuable lesson. He said to him:

> I entered your house; you gave Me no water for My feet, but she has wet My feet with her tears, and wiped them with her hair. You gave Me no kiss; but she, since the time I came in, has not ceased to kiss My feet. You did

not anoint My head with oil, but she anointed My feet with perfume." ... And He said to her, "Your sins have been forgiven" (Luke 7:36-48).

In Matthew 26:13, Jesus pays tribute to this woman who served him, saying, "Truly I say to you, wherever this gospel is preached in the whole world, what this woman has done shall also be spoken of in memory of her." And so it is today, some 2,000 years later, that wherever in the world the Bible is read, we still remember her kind, compassionate acts of service.

NOWHERE TO LAY HIS HEAD

On one occasion, Jesus was preparing to go to Jerusalem. He sent messengers ahead of Him to make arrangements for His arrival. But when they entered a village of the Samaritans, they would not receive Him because "He was journeying with His face toward Jerusalem" (Luke 9:53). James and John were indignant. Living up to their nickname, the Sons of Thunder, they asked Jesus, "Lord, do You want us to command fire to come down from heaven and consume them?" (v. 54).

For this impulsive reaction, Jesus turned and rebuked them. Later as they traveled on to another village, Jesus made this poignant observation: "The foxes have holes, and the birds of the air have nests, but the Son of Man has nowhere to lay His head" (Luke 9:58).

Although Jesus was often denied hospitality, He did extend hospitality to others. On the morning after His disciples had fished all night and had caught nothing, Jesus called to them to cast their nets on the other side of the boat. When they did, they caught so many fish they could not pull the nets back into the boat. They pulled them onto the shore and found Jesus on the beach with a fire already made and fish cooking and bread baking on the hot stones. He had prepared breakfast for the hungry fishermen.

MISSING THE OPPORTUNITY TO FORGIVE

Contrast the woman at Simon's house with the actions of the prodigal's older brother. We noted earlier in Chapter 8 how the father of the prodigal extended loving hospitality to his wayward son. But when the older brother heard the sounds of the welcoming party, he asked a servant what was going on.

He was informed that his younger brother had returned and a feast had been prepared to welcome him. Jealousy and anger engulfed him and wiped away all thoughts of celebration. "For so many years I have been serving you, and I have never neglected a command of yours; and yet you have never given me a kid, that I might be merry with my friends" (Luke 15:29). He missed an opportunity to forgive, to offer hospitality, and to reunite with his brother.

DENYING HOSPITALITY TO THE POOR

Jesus had a heart of compassion for the poor because they are often the ones overlooked or cast aside. When He came into Nazareth and entered the synagogue, He was handed the book of Isaiah to read. He opened the book and found this prophecy: "The Spirit of the Lord is upon Me, Because He anointed Me to preach the gospel to the poor. He has sent Me to proclaim release to the captives, And recovery of sight To the blind, to set free those who are downtrodden" (Luke 4:18).

Often these people – the destitute, the disenfranchised and the downtrodden – are overlooked when we think of hospitality. In the book of Luke we read the story Jesus told about a rich man who denied hospitality to the poor.

> Now there was a certain rich man, and he habitually dressed in purple and fine linen, gaily living in splendor every day. And a certain poor man named Lazarus was laid at his gate, covered with sores, and longing to be fed with the crumbs which were falling from the rich man's table; besides, even the dogs were coming and licking his sores (Luke 16:19-21).

The rich man had only to go outside his own gate to find one in dire need, but he denied the man hospitality.

Solomon wrote, "He who oppresses the poor reproaches his Maker, But he who is gracious to the needy honors Him" (Proverbs 14:31). "He who is gracious to a poor man lends to the Lord, And He will repay him for his good deed" (19:17).

God doesn't require us to eliminate all poverty. That would be an impossible task. But we are to help people as we are given opportunity. "So then, while we have opportunity, let us do good to all men, and especially to those who are of the household of the faith" (Galatians 6:10).

QUESTIONS
1. What were some of the customs of hospitality to guests in Jesus' time?

2. When was Jesus denied hospitality?

3. How was Simon, the Pharisee, an inhospitable host?

4. How did Jesus compliment the sinful woman who anointed Him?

5. What was Jesus' attitude toward the poor?

SMALL GROUP DISCUSSION
1. How would you explain the difference between the teaching in Matthew 6:1-4 and Matthew 5:16?

2. What are the opportunities in your community for helping the poor?

A KIND WORD

"A child should always say what's true
And speak when he is spoken to,
And behave mannerly at table;
At least as far as he is able."
Robert Lewis Stevenson

"The child is father of the man."
William Wordsworth

"Even a child is known by his doings, whether his work
is pure, and whether it be right" (Proverbs 20:11 KJV).

CHAPTER 12

TEACHING CHILDREN HOSPITALITY

"Train up a child in the way he should go, even when he is old he will not depart from it" (Proverbs 22:6).

As mentioned in Chapter 1, mentoring children is one of the benefits of hospitality. Human beings are basically selfish creatures. We are not born with a hospitality gene, so it is up to parents to teach this attribute to their children.

An important facet of hospitality is the knowledge and use of good manners. Basically, using good manners is a way of putting the Golden Rule into practice. "Whatsoever ye would that men should do to you, do ye even so to them" (Matthew 7:12 KJV).

When I was a child, friends would gather in our neighborhood to play games like "Red Rover" or "Dodge Ball." One game I remember was "Mother, May I?" It was similar to the game "Simon Says," but before following a command – such as "stand on one foot" or "touch your toes" – a player would have to first ask, "Mother, may I?" Neglecting to remember this phrase would send a player back to the end of the line. I suspect this was the clever invention of some long-ago mother who was trying to encourage politeness in her children.

Emily Post, a long-time advisor on proper etiquette, stated her philosophy toward etiquette: "Manners was made up of trivialities of deportment which can be easily learned if one does not happen to know them; manner is personality – the outward manifestation of one's innate character and attitude toward life."

She emphasized that a child learns proper etiquette by watching the example of his or her mother: "A really charming woman exerts her charm nowhere more than upon her husband and children, and a noble nature through daily though unconscious example is of course the greatest influence for good that there is in the world."

This is where we first learn manners: at home, where we watch how our mothers and fathers relate to others; and secondly, by the things they teach us. To help them learn hospitality, we should teach our children about the etiquette of mealtimes, of respect for others, and respect for the property of others.

ETIQUETTE OF MEALTIMES

When our children were small, we would coach them on the behavior we expected of them before entering a restaurant or someone's home for dinner. We reminded them to stay in their chairs during dinner, to say "please" and "thank you," and to chew with their mouths closed. Of course, there were the more basic admonitions such as, "Don't put your hand in your water glass!"

Anticipating problem areas ahead of time is much better than having to dole out constant reprimands at the table in the presence of other guests. Here are some examples of what we should teach our children about mealtimes.

• Do not hurry to be the first in line at potluck dinners, but "give preference to one another in honor" (Romans 12:10). Wait patiently in line, and offer to let another go ahead of you.

• When seated at a dinner, do not start eating until everyone at your table has been served. The same applies at dessert time. The exception would be at a large banquet, in which case, wait until at least two people on either side of you have been served. If you are the only one waiting for your plate, encourage others to start.

• Teach your children to try new foods or simply say, "No thank you" rather than, "I don't like that!"

RESPECT FOR OTHERS

When my husband is introduced to a small boy, he often teaches him how to shake hands properly. He tells them to do three things: "Number one: Look me in the eye. Number two: Smile. And number three: Give me a firm handshake."

The point of knowing etiquette is to feel comfortable in social situations and to make others feel comfortable around us, not to use it as one-upmanship. In fact, if each could learn only one rule of etiquette – the biblical principle of putting others first – this one principle would serve us well whether at a backyard barbeque or dinner at the White House.

The purpose of etiquette is not to promote snobbishness ("Excuse me, but you're using the wrong fork") but to help social situations run smoothly. We should overlook another's error in the hopes that we will be treated as kindly when we inevitably make mistakes of our own.

We should teach our children that R.S.V.P. on a formal invitation is an abbreviation for the French *répondez s'il vous plaît*, or please respond, and that they should let the person know if they are planning to accept the invitation. Not doing so is disrespectful and leaves the hostess not knowing how many to plan for and perhaps not able to invite another guest in your place.

The Bible gives examples of putting others first and respecting others. "Do nothing from selfishness or empty conceit, but with humility of mind let each of you regard one another as more important than himself" (Philippians 2:3). "Honor all men" (1 Peter 2:17). We must be friendly with those who are different from us. "And if you greet your brothers only, what do you do more than others? Do not even the Gentiles do the same?" (Matthew 5:47).

When Jesus was invited to the home of an important Pharisee for a meal, he observed that some were choosing the best places for themselves. He took this opportunity to teach a valuable lesson in the form of a parable:

> When you are invited by someone to a wedding feast, do not take the place of honor, lest someone more distinguished than you may have been invited by him, and

he who invited you both shall come and say to you, "Give place to this man," and then in disgrace you proceed to occupy the last place.

But when you are invited, go and recline at the last place, so that when the one who has invited you comes, he may say to you, "Friend, move up higher"; then you will have honor in the sight of all who are at the table with you. For everyone who exalts himself shall be humbled, and he who humbles himself shall be exalted" (Luke 14:11).

Another etiquette expert, Amy Vanderbilt, stated, "[I am] a journalist in the field of etiquette. I try to find out what the most genteel people regularly do, what traditions they have discarded, what compromises they have made."

Customs of etiquette vary from country to country and from generation to generation. The rules are not the important things in themselves, but the thought behind them is what matters. Let that thought be this: whatever I can do to make myself a welcome guest or welcoming hostess, let me do my best.

RESPECT FOR THE PROPERTY OF OTHERS

One of the first lessons God taught Adam was to take care of the property He had given them. "Then the LORD God took the man and put him into the garden of Eden to cultivate it and keep it" (Genesis 2:15).

At a state conference of Keep Tennessee Beautiful, Dr. George Kelling spoke about the importance of respecting property. Dr. Kelling, author of *Fixing Broken Windows*, is a criminologist who had the idea that crime is caused by disorder. Disorderly conduct is a sign that no one cares. If you leave just a small thing like a broken window, it invites another window to be broken. A trashy street keeps the law-abiding citizens from going there. It invites the small crimes and makes people fearful. If this is not corrected, bigger crimes result and the problem snowballs.

In 1989, Dr. Kelling was hired by the New York Transit Authority as a consultant, and he put the "Broken Windows" theory into practice. First they cleaned up graffiti on the subway cars, and kept them clean. Next they cracked down on those who didn't pay their subway fares.

The result was that not only was disorderly conduct in subways stopped, but there was also more than a 50 percent decrease in harder crimes in the first year alone, and an 80 percent reduction in years that followed. His theory was proven. Minor, seemingly insignificant quality-of-life crimes were tipping points for violent crime.

It would seem to follow that these smaller crimes could similarly be prevented by teaching our children to respect the property of others. Mothers and fathers who teach their children to take care of songbooks during worship and not to write on pews or classroom desks and walls are setting the stage for respecting the property of others. Teaching simple manners at home – keeping feet off the furniture, placing litter in trash cans instead of dropping it on the ground, and picking clothes up off the floor – will help children learn that respecting property of others is a way of showing respect for the people who own the property.

FINDING THE RIGHT WORDS

• *"I'm sorry."* A line from the 1970 movie *Love Story* suggested, "Love means never having to say you're sorry." But does it really? Teaching our children to apologize for hurting someone or breaking something is a way of showing good manners, but more important, it teaches them to feel remorse and repentance for their mistakes and wrongdoing.

• *"Thank you."* Another biblical principle that is stressed in any book of manners is that of showing gratitude. Thankfulness toward the giver of a gift or some service rendered is a sign of good etiquette.

"[I]n everything give thanks; for this is God's will for you in Christ Jesus" (1 Thessalonians 5:18). "[G]iving thanks for all things in the name of our Lord Jesus Christ" (Ephesians 5:20).

Jesus taught about remembering to say thank you.

And as He entered a certain village, ten leprous men who stood at a distance met Him; and they raised their voices, saying, "Jesus, Master, have mercy on us!" And when He saw them, He said to them, "Go and show yourselves to the priests." And it came about that as they were going, they were cleansed. Now one of them, when he saw that he had been healed, turned back, glorifying God with a loud voice, and he fell on his face at His feet, giving thanks to Him. And he was a Samaritan. And Jesus answered and said, "Were there not ten cleansed? But the nine – where are they? Was no one found who turned back to give glory to God, except this foreigner?" (Luke 17:12-18).

Jesus taught also by His own example. After feeding the multitudes, Jesus did not wait for people to thank Him, but instead, "He took the seven loaves and the fish; and giving thanks, He broke them and started giving them to the disciples, and the disciples in turn, to the multitudes" (Matthew 15:36).

THE WISDOM OF SCRIPTURES

I see many young women in the church training their children to be mannerly, and they are to be commended. One young mother in particular has impressed me with her attention to this part of her children's training. Lisa Reese, a young, conscientious mother in Alabama, is developing a program for use with her children and those of her friends to teach proper etiquette in meeting people, in use of the telephone, and at mealtimes.

Lisa's instruction is based on the wisdom of the scriptures. She cites the teaching of King Lemuel and the instruction his mother gave to him:

> What, O my son? And what, O son of my womb? And what, O son of my vows? Do not give your strength to women, Or your ways to that which destroys kings. It is not for kings, O Lemuel, It is not for kings to drink wine, Or for rulers to desire strong drink, Lest they drink and forget what is decreed, And pervert the rights of all the afflicted. Give strong drink to him who is perishing And wine to him whose life is bitter. Let him drink and

forget his poverty, And remember his trouble no more. Open your mouth for the dumb, For the rights of all the unfortunate. Open your mouth, judge righteously, And defend the rights of the afflicted and needy (Proverbs 31:2-10).

Lemuel's mother was preparing her son to be a king. It is interesting to note that she was also concerned that he should develop a benevolent spirit, with a heart of compassion for the needy.

Here are a few points in some of the units Lisa is teaching her children:

- *Week One: Meeting and Greeting Others*

1. A happy countenance: "A joyful heart makes a cheerful face" (Proverbs 15:13). Manners are very important when you are meeting someone for the first time.

2. Showing honor: "You shall rise up before the grayheaded, and honor the aged, and you shall revere your God; I am the Lord" (Leviticus 19:32). Always stand up when being introduced to someone. It is respectful to older persons, when they enter a room, that you help them find a seat. It may even necessitate that you give them your seat, and you stand or sit in the floor.

"Do not claim honor in the presence of the king, And do not stand in the place of great men; For it is better that it be said to you, 'Come up here,' Than that you should be put lower in the presence of the prince, Whom your eyes have seen" (Proverbs 25:6-7).

3. Introductions and conversation: "Render to all what is due them ... honor to whom honor" (Romans 13:7). Remember to be a good listener. Do not brag. When you brag, you are showing off in words. "Let another praise you, and not your own mouth" (Proverbs 27:2).

Find positive things to say about others. "Let no unwholesome word proceed from your mouth, but only such a word as is good for edification according to the need of the moment, that it may give grace to those who hear" (Ephesians 4:29).

Along with this unit, Lisa has the children practice giving introductions, giving praise to someone else, shaking hands, and saying "please" and "thank you." She lets them make simple crafts to reinforce the lessons and helps them put together a small booklet containing a checklist of do's and don'ts.

• *Week Two: Telephone Manners*

Teach about avoiding gossip and telling the truth. "A perverse man spreads strife, And a slanderer separates intimate friends" (Proverbs 16:28).

• *Week Three: Good Hosts, Good Guests*

Teach about having guests and being a good guest with age-appropriate reminders to "Wipe your feet before entering someone's home" or "Keep your voice down low, never yell," and "Ask before getting out a toy, and put it back before getting another one to play with."

• *Week Four: Writing Thank You Notes*

Children learn to make their own note cards with stamped designs and write a simple thank you message.

In Lisa's teaching of manners to her children, she also provides opportunity for her children to be of service to others. For instance, one of the older ladies at church was overheard wishing for a pillow to put behind her back for comfort during church services. That week Lisa purchased fabric, sewed pillows and let her daughters stuff them. The joy these girls received from giving them to the older ladies was a great reward. They learned to give the gifts of service and comfort.

You can imagine, with this kind of time and effort and planning with her three children, they are a delight to be around. Besides the Bible, Lisa uses as a resource a book by Emilie Barnes, *A Little Book of Manners* (Harvest House Publishers, 1998).

CHILDREN OF THE KING

Our children are the children of a king, as are we. It is worth the time and effort we expend in teaching our children to be respectful of other people and their property. This is teaching them to observe the second greatest commandment: "[L]ove your neighbor as yourself" (Leviticus 19:18).

Children learn how to serve by watching the example of their parents. Colleen DeLoach of Fayetteville, Ark., shared what she learned by watching her mother, Mollie Jordan. "My mother has been my greatest example of showing hospitality. She doesn't wait for opportunities to present themselves, she looks for opportunities. Her service is well known in the little town where they live. She cooks and delivers more meals than I can imagine. She visits the sick and those in nursing homes. I've seen her care for many of my elderly relatives. She gives the same care to in-laws that she does to her own flesh and blood. She has helped neighbors and strangers. She has truly been my example of what it is to be a servant."

Now, Colleen is following in her mother's footsteps as she and her husband, Steve, are part of Partners in Progress serving in Guyana, South America. My husband and I saw firsthand how this medical mission effort offers hospitality to the Guyanese. They coordinate teams of Christians from the United States to take medical care to those who are ill, build church buildings and pews, provide counseling on sanitation and first aid, supply clothing and food, conduct Bible studies with individuals, and nurture existing congregations of the Lord's people in Guyana. Never underestimate the far-reaching effects of the example you set before your children.

"Let your father and your mother be glad, And let her rejoice who gave birth to you" (Proverbs 23:25).

QUESTIONS

1. What does the Bible teach about manners?

2. What is the importance of using good manners?

3. How can we show honor to others through our use of good manners?

4. What does Matthew 5:47 teach us about manners?

SMALL GROUP DISCUSSION

1. How did you teach your children to observe good manners at the table?

2. What are some manners that children should be taught to observe in the church building?

3. What are some of the rules of etiquette you expect of yourself when you visit a home?

4. What do you appreciate in others when they are guests in your home?

A KIND WORD

"God never sendeth mouth but He sendeth meat."
John Heywood

"Let not your heart be troubled; believe in God,
believe also in Me. In My Father's house are
many dwelling places; if it were not so, I would
have told you; for I go to prepare a place for you.
And if I go and prepare a place for you, I will
come again, and receive you to Myself; that where
I am, there you may be also" (John 14:1-3).

CHAPTER 13

GOD'S GIFTS OF HOSPITALITY TO CHRISTIANS

"For by grace you have been saved through faith; and that not of yourselves, it is the gift of God" (Ephesians 2:8).

The writer of Hebrews recounts many disobedient actions of the children of Israel that caused them to miss entering the promised land of Canaan. "Therefore, let us fear lest, while a promise remains of entering His rest, any one of you should seem to have come short of it" (Hebrews 4:1).

Jesus teaches that some people will miss heaven's hospitality through their own negligence.

> Then the kingdom of heaven will be comparable to ten virgins, who took their lamps, and went out to meet the bridegroom. And five of them were foolish, and five were prudent. For when the foolish took their lamps, they took no oil with them, but the prudent took oil in flasks along with their lamps. Now while the bridegroom was delaying, they all got drowsy and began to sleep. But at midnight there was a shout, "Behold, the bridegroom! Come out to meet him." Then all those virgins rose, and trimmed their lamps. And the foolish said to the prudent, "Give us some of your oil, for our lamps

122 of HOSPITALITY TO CHRISTIANS

are going out." But the prudent answered, saying, "No, there will not be enough for us and you too; go instead to the dealers and buy some for yourselves."

And while they were going away to make the purchase, the bridegroom came, and those who were ready went in with him to the wedding feast; and the door was shut. And later the other virgins also came, saying, "Lord, lord, open up for us."

But he answered and said, "Truly I say to you, I do not know you" (Matthew 25:1-12).

GOD'S INVITATION

God wants His house to be full of those who accept His invitation. "The Lord is not slow about His promise, as some count slowness, but is patient toward you, not wishing for any to perish but for all to come to repentance" (2 Peter 3:9).

He told His disciples a parable about a man giving a big dinner party and inviting many guests. When the day came, he sent his slave to tell the people to come in because everything was prepared and ready for them. But to his dismay, the guests began to make excuses. One found it necessary to check on a piece of real estate he had just purchased. Another had purchased five yoke of oxen and was anxious to try them out. Yet a third guest said, "I have married a wife, and for that reason I cannot come" (Luke 14:20).

When this was reported to the master, he was very angry. Had he not spent time, money and effort in preparing this feast? Were they not appreciative? Couldn't their other obligations wait until a later time?

The master then told his slave to go into the streets of the city and bring in the poor, crippled and blind. After doing this, there still was room. The master sent the slave out again, saying, "Go out into the highways and along the hedges, and compel them to come in, that my house may be filled. For I tell you, none of those men who were invited shall taste of my dinner" (Luke 14:23-24).

The message for us is to appreciate God's invitation and be prepared to accept it in order to enjoy His hospitality eternally.

> But since we are of the day, let us be sober, having put on the breastplate of faith and love, and as a helmet, the hope of salvation. For God has not destined us for wrath, but for obtaining salvation through our Lord Jesus Christ, who died for us, that whether we are awake or asleep, we may live together with Him (1 Thessalonians 5:8-10).

THINGS THAT ACCOMPANY SALVATION

In reading the last will and testament of Jesus, we learn many things that accompany the inheritance of salvation.

> But, beloved, we are convinced of better things concerning you, and things that accompany salvation, though we are speaking in this way. For God is not unjust so as to forget your work and the love which you have shown toward His name, in having ministered and in still ministering to the saints. And we desire that each one of you show the same diligence so as to realize the full assurance of hope until the end (Hebrews 6:9-11).

We learn that we should deny ourselves and take up our crosses and follow Him (Matthew 16:24). We learn that people will know us as His disciples if we have love one for another (John 13:35). We learn that anyone who does not practice righteousness is not of God (1 John 3:10). And we learn that we must give up our possessions to look after the needs of others: "So therefore, no one of you can be My disciple who does not give up all his own possessions" (Luke 14:33). "If a brother or sister is without clothing and in need of daily food, and one of you says to them, 'Go in peace, be warmed and be filled,' and yet you do not give them what is necessary for their body, what use is that?" (James 2:15-16).

When we offer gifts of hospitality to others, we are, in effect, showing this same hospitality to the Lord and doing as He would have done. "[T]he one who says he abides in Him ought himself to walk in the same manner as He walked" (1 John 2:6).

ENDURING GIFTS

God's love for us is overwhelming, and in His generous nature He offers gifts of hospitality beyond the physical. His gifts are enduring and everlasting. He does not require of us that which He does not willingly give. The following passages tell of His gifts to Christians:

1. The gift of nourishment: "He who has an ear, let him hear what the Spirit says to the churches. To him who overcomes, I will grant to eat of the tree of life, which is in the Paradise of God" (Revelation 2:7).

2. The gift of service: "Jesus stood and cried out, saying, 'If any man is thirsty, let him come to me and drink. He who believes in me, as the Scripture said, From his innermost being shall flow rivers of living water'" (John 7:37-38).

3. The gift of shelter: "Let not your heart be troubled; believe in God, believe also in Me. In My Father's house are many dwelling places; if it were not so, I would have told you; for I go to prepare a place for you. And if I go and prepare a place for you, I will come again, and receive you to Myself; that where I am, there you may be also (John 14:1-3).

4. The gift of benevolence: We will wear robes of white, washed in the blood of the Lamb. "'These who are clothed in the white robes, who are they, and from where have they come?' And I said to him, 'My lord, you know.' And he said to me, 'These are the ones who come out of the great tribulation, and they have washed their robes and made them white in the blood of the Lamb'" (Revelation 7:13-14).

5. The gift of comfort: "And He shall wipe away every tear from their eyes; and there shall no longer be any death; there shall no longer be any mourning, or crying, or pain; the first things have passed away" (Revelation 21:4).

6. The gift of companionship: "He who overcomes shall inherit these things, and I will be his God and he will be My son" (Revelation 21:7). "For He hath said, I will never leave thee, nor forsake thee" (Hebrews 13:5 KJV).

The psalmist, David, wrote about God's hospitality in Psalm 23:

The Lord is my shepherd,
I shall not want (*the gift of benevolence*).
He makes me lie down in green pastures;
He leads me beside quiet waters.
He restores my soul (*the gift of comfort.*)
He guides me in the paths of righteousness
For His name's sake (*the gift of service*).
Even though I walk through the valley of the shadow
    of death,
I fear no evil; for Thou art with me (*the gift of companionship*).
Thy rod and Thy staff, they comfort me.
Thou dost prepare a table before me in the presence
    of my enemies (*the gift of nourishment*).
Thou hast anointed my head with oil;
My cup overflows.
Surely goodness and lovingkindness will follow me all
    the days of my life,
And I will dwell in the house of the Lord forever (*the gift of shelter*)

ETERNAL HOSPITALITY

Our reward for offering hospitality to others is eternal hospitality with God in His kingdom.

Then the King will say to those on His right, "Come, you who are blessed of My Father, inherit the kingdom prepared for you from the foundation of the world.

"For I was hungry, and you gave Me something to eat; I was thirsty, and you gave Me drink; I was a stranger, and you invited Me in; naked, and you clothed Me; I was sick, and you visited Me; I was in prison, and you came to Me" (Matthew 25:34-36).

The people would ask when did they see Jesus naked and hungry and the King would answer them, "Truly I say to you, to the extent that you did it to one of these brothers of Mine, even the least of them, you did it to Me" (Matthew 25:40).

QUESTIONS

1. What caused the Israelites to miss God's hospitality in the land of Canaan?

2. What are some things that accompany salvation?

3. What might cause us to miss out on God's invitation?

4. How will God show His hospitality to the faithful?

SMALL GROUP DISCUSSION

1. In reflecting upon the lessons in this book, in what areas of hospitality do you feel most confident?

2. Are there areas of your hospitality that you would like to improve?

3. What questions regarding the six gifts of hospitality would you like to discuss with others in your class?

LISTEN CHRISTIAN

I was hungry
> and you formed a humanities club
> and discussed my hunger.
> Thank you.

I was imprisoned
> and you crept off
> quietly in your chapel
> in the cellar and prayed my release.

I was naked
> and in your mind you debated
> the morality of my appearance.

I was sick
> and you knelt and thanked God for your
> health.

I was homeless
> and you preached to me of the
> spiritual shelter of the love of God.

I was lonely
> and you left me alone to pray for me.

You seem so holy; so close to God
> but I'm still very hungry,
> and lonely,
> and cold.

Bob Rowland

RESOURCES

Earle, Ralph. *Adam Clarke's Commentary on the Bible*, Abridged. Iowa Falls, Iowa: World Bible Publishers, Inc., 1967.

Kelling, George L. and Catherine M. Coles. *Fixing Broken Windows: Restoring Order and Reducing Crime in our Communities*. New York: Simon and Schuster, 1997.

Knott, Ronald Alan, ed. *College Faith*. Berrien Springs, Michigan: Andrews University Press, 2002.

Powell, Alvin. "Putting a Dollar Value on a Good Name." *Harvard University Gazette*. Harvard University Office of News and Public Affairs, 22 July 2003. www.news.harvard. edu/gazette/2003/02.27-ebay.html.

Simpson, Peggy. *Hospitality: In the Spirit of Love*. Abilene, Texas: Quality Publications, 1980.

U.S. Department of Health and Human Services, Office on Women's Health, http://www.4woman.gov/COE/third.htm

U.S. Department of Health and Human Services, Administration on Aging, http://www.aoa.dhhs.gov/May2000/FactSheets/ CaregiverSupport2000.html